Having had the pleasure of working with Morrighan and speaking with her at length I know what a special human being she is, and have seen how she shares her bright spirit with others. She feels. She honors. She gives. If you are open, or even just a little curious, I highly recommend this read. Morrighan has put together a spiritual master class on being your best self. Trust you have found yourself here for a reason and go on this journey with her, as it will set you off on your own true journey that will last a lifetime.

Carrie Genzel – Actor & Creator/Writer of State Of Slay

If you are searching for a way to expand all that you are, this is where you begin. Morrighan is an amazing storyteller. Her words drew me in and wouldn't let go! Not only are these techniques vital in today's society but Morrighan has found a way to explain the abstract and put it into applicable, relatable terminology. A must read!

David Joyner – Actor, Entertainer/Original Barney, Tantra Massage Specialist & Spiritual Energy Healer

What do we choose to obscure from ourselves and the world? This book takes the seeker on an archeological expedition of self-exploration. Uncovering revelations of our hidden selves with every turned page. Fascinating read!

Barbara Mackey – Internationally known Psychic /Medium, TV & Radio Celebrity

The Spirited Human

the Spirited Human

PROACTIVE TOOLS FOR A REACTIVE WORLD

MORRIGHAN LYNNE

929 Publishing

6568 S Federal Way
#319
Boise, ID 83716

Ladies and gentlemen, the stories you are about to read are true. Only the names have been changed to protect the innocent and the facts have been changed to protect the guilty.

Library of Congress Cataloging-in-Publication Data is available

10 9 8 7 6 5 4 3 2

Printed in the United States

ISBN 978-0-9997779-9-2

With deepest gratitude...

I wouldn't be the girl I am today if it hadn't been for you:

My Guardian Angels & Spirit Guides, Archangel Michael,
The Morrighan, The Big O, and The Eight.

Thank you for never giving up on me.

I love you.

♥

Contents

Foreword

The cosmos are alive and vibrating and within those vibrations infinite possibilities await. Faced with this realization wouldn't it be nice if someone wrote a book to teach people how to tap into those vibrations to help humanity? Well, that's exactly what Morrighan has done with her delightful and insightful book, *The Spirited Human!* In this book, she offers practical tips and tools for navigating the world of the unknown, towards personal growth and development.

We have run a successful improvisational comedy club, Four Day Weekend, for the last twenty years and the insights Morrighan provides, within these pages, align with our very positive, forward-thinking approach to life and business.

In improvisation, we are constantly stepping into the unknown, and facing challenges, without fear. It's like life - we don't know where we're going, we only know where we've been. We are able to fearlessly step into the unknown when we realize that these challenges are what make life interesting and fun. We should always embrace these things, instead of running from them, and this book shows you how to do that.

In our world of improvisation, when we align with each other in unity what we come up with together is far better than what we come up with individually and when we honor those around us we are honored in return. These principles are the very same principles that have guided Morrighan on her path of guiding and healing people during this new age of consciousness.

Morrighan challenges us to approach our lives with an open mind and be aware of everything around us. Her humor, story and advice help us to look within ourselves, and others, to achieve a Higher Good. At the end of the day, isn't that what humanity is all about?

Read this book and take the first step towards creating a kinder and more compassionate world. As Morrighan's insightful book reveals, when we acknowledge everything in the Universe everything acknowledges us in return. Let us all strive to become The Spirited Human and together we will transform the world.

Foreword by David Ahearn & Frank Ford
Co-Authors of the National Bestseller, *Happy Accidents*
Co-Founders of Four Day Weekend Comedy

Spirited: /ˈspiridəd/

Full of energy, enthusiasm, courage, and determination.

Human: /ˈ(h)yo͞omən/

Relating to or characteristic of people or human beings.

The Spirited Human:

A person courageous enough to ask the bigger questions, willing to
hear the truer answers, and daring enough to go beyond their
comfort zone in order to have all that they came here to be.
It is the brave soul daring to be amazing!

Breadcrumbs

As I pondered what to title this maiden voyage of mine, I found it difficult to land on the perfect juxtaposition between the spiritual heart and the pragmatic head. If I went in the direction of my own personal beliefs, it would be so "ooey-gooey spiritual" that it might turn away those that didn't use the same language. And yet if I took a more logical route, it would swing too far away from my own truth as a person who walks a spiritual path.

For months, I struggled to strike just the right balance. But as with all moments in my life where I lack clarity, I just trusted and pressed on. I wrote what I knew and knew what I didn't would come in its own time. Then suddenly, one day *boom* it finally appeared! For me, this title speaks of the human in action, facing their fears and slaying their dragons; being courageous and determined in their quest to know self. I'm happy to present to you, my first baby:

The Spirited Human: Proactive Tools for a Reactive World!

I wrote this book with the human in mind. Not the spiritual human. Not the religious human. And not any other human with any other label, status, or classification attached to it. I wrote it for humanity. We are all designed the same way. Each and every one of us was born with the systems I talk about in these pages. Just as we all have the same organs, cells, and tissues, we all have the same subtle systems within our field. And those systems are in need of maintenance to keep them properly running.

Implementing the tools shared in this book will have no bearing on where you place your faith, how you pray, or in which manner you worship the Divine. It isn't a dogma, theology, or any particular ideology. These practices are for maintenance. Pure and simple. What is listed in this book are the tools that allow you, the reactionary, free will human, to be proactive in your own life. The intention is to offer a resource to assist you in taking responsibility for your experience, empowering that part of you that sometimes feels victimized and beaten down. There is no belief system here. Only an invitation, some education, and potentially a new course for your life.

As you read through these chapters, I'm asking you, even daring you, to be open-minded about what is being offered. As I'm sure my clients would attest, working with me will at times make you feel uncomfortable. I'll more than likely talk of things that you'll want to reject. I may bring to the forefront conversations that possibly don't travel in your social groups. You might even find yourself questioning years of programming that was handed down to you as a young person.

And isn't that delicious?! Why not go beyond what you know? Why wouldn't you question everything? What would be possible for you if you went past your comfort zone and reached out into the unexplored? If anything, life *should* be about the adventure. Being a spirited human is all about daring to go into the farthest reaches of our knowing and understanding. It's about taking that big, beautiful leap into the sea of possibility and exploring the deep unknown. So, welcome brave soul! Welcome to this new fork in the road less traveled. Welcome to the adventure that is yours!

"My Guys"

I have this interesting relationship with these incredibly sarcastic Divine beings. They are my angels, spirit guides, and teachers, and they are pretty freaking fabulous! They are the ones I lovingly call my Guys. I call them that because they like to keep it casual. There's no need to sing sonnets or recite special prayers to converse with them. They're humble and loving, completely trustworthy, and can be snarky at times. They've even been known to drop the F-bomb here and there if you can believe that.

As close as we are now, it's hard to believe I didn't like them much in the beginning. In fact, I did everything I could to reject them! In my ignorance, I thought they were there to judge me and steer me towards a specific religious teaching. At that point in my life, I was still very much searching for my own beliefs and not those that were handed down to me.

So, when they showed up wanting to talk with me, I wouldn't have anything to do with them. I pushed them away and rejected their support. Being the quintessential Aries, I was determined to do it all on my own. It wasn't until I stopped being so ignorant and resistant that I realized they just wanted to love and support me, right where I was, with whatever I wanted to do in life.

What I have come to appreciate over the years is their willingness to nudge, whisper, teach, and yes sometimes, even kick me in the pants when I need it. I used to tease that one of my angels had a two-by-four that he would use upside my head when I just wasn't getting it. It may have knocked me around here and there but honestly, I needed it.

Because let's face it, humans are stubborn! If we don't know how the story ends, we won't take a single step forward until we are sure it is a viable investment of our time. We want things the way we want them and will put so much effort into it that we can lose sight of our initial intention. We get extremely attached to the outcome we desire. When it doesn't work out the way we expect, it shakes our faith. Disappointment sets in, and we begin to question all that we know. So much effort, force, and control just to dictate our end result. It's exhausting! And rather boring to be honest.

XVII

Breadcrumbs

Our guides, however, take a different approach. They understand we want the easy answer, but that isn't always the best route to take. Rather than rushing towards the punchline, they allow the story to play out. This gives us the full-meal-deal! They offer clues and insights, piece by piece so to not take away the surprise at the end.

Basically, the role of our guides is to assist us in getting to the destination that we decided long before we were born. Our soul has a plan and it navigates through life with an overall goal in mind. Even though we are born without memories of those plans, our guides do, however, remember. Therefore, the soul contract is to be our "travel companions" and help us eventually find our way without giving away all the answers.

My Guys call it the breadcrumb trail. Piece by piece, they offer us clues that lead us in the direction we originally wanted to go. A nudge here, an insight there. One at a time, showing pieces of a puzzle that eventually starts to bring the journey into clear view. And even though they commit to not giving the answers away, they do enjoy watching us find the clues and figuring it out for ourselves.

You might be asking, "Why don't they just tell us the answer?" Think about Christmas morning as a kid, coming downstairs after Santa has visited your house and seeing all the presents under the tree. If your parents were to tell you what was in each of those boxes before you got to rip them open, it would completely take the joy out of the experience, right? That's how our guides work. They don't want to give away the good stuff. It's such a joy for them to watch us shake the gift and try to guess, and then rip open the paper to see if we were right. Why would they ruin the best part for us?

Instead, they simply honor us, right where we are, but with little nudges from time to time that will get us heading in the right direction. We have total free will. We can say no to their offerings. We can choose other paths. We can even refuse their support. But that will never change what our soul initially said it wanted to experience. And our guides are just there to help us get on track with those initial plans.

House on a Hill

A term I use quite often throughout these pages is shadow (as in shadow work, shadow self, shadow ego, you get the picture). I want to take a moment to explain just what this means to me, because anytime I use this term, people tend to react in a fearful way. The general response is that of disgust, as if a demon is about to come suck out their soul, and we had all better run and hide before it appears. No. Just no. Using the term "shadow" has nothing to do with evil, bad, or demonic forces. Shadow simply means the aspects and traits that we hide away so that we don't have to deal with them. They are the pieces and parts of us that are wounded and in need of healing. We shove them down so we can act as if they do not exist, hiding them in the shadows, hoping no one will find them and be horrified by our ugliness. Sometimes, we hide them because we are ashamed. Other times, we just stuff them down so we can push on in life. Regardless, our shadow is still a part of us. And in our quest for wholeness, we cannot deny our shadow and focus only on the light. Celebrating what is good, but hating what we think is bad does not create a balanced human.

"To confront a person with his shadow is to show him his own light. Once one has experienced a few times what it is like to stand judgingly between the opposites, one begins to understand what is meant by the self. Anyone who perceives his shadow and his light simultaneously sees himself from two sides and thus gets in the middle."
- Carl Jung

Imagine, if you will, that you live in a beautiful house on a hill. Everything is in its place, perfect and immaculate. Not a single speck of dust. Except you keep throwing your garbage in the basement. Yes, it may be out of sight and out of mind, but eventually the smell will start to creep into your home. Ignore it, and it will start to mildew and stink even more. Ignore it even further, and the foundation of the home begins to rot until eventually it collapses on top of you.

Shadow work is about being brave enough to open the basement doors and to simply see what's down there. It's about being willing to sift through the bags of trash and pull out anything that is still useful. Not everything we throw away is garbage. We sometimes throw away beautiful things, valuable things in our haste to move away from the hurt. So we sift, we dig, we acknowledge, and we salvage what is still valuable. Then, we can properly dispose of the waste that is no longer needed. This is how I see shadow work. It is not dangerous. It is not harmful. For me, it's where our true foundation resides. Down in the dark, digging deep into our souls and excavating what needs our acknowledgment. This courageous act of caring for our wounds is what allows them to be fully healed. There is nothing braver than a soul willing to open those doors.

Knock, Knock

I had to open this door, not only for me, but to help you open yours. Writing this book has been quite the labor of love, I'll admit. When my guides came to me in 2008 with the announcement that they "had my first book for me," I rejected their offer. What they meant by their statement was they were going to assist me in writing a book by downloading me with information that was pertinent to share at that time. But I have a tendency to veer away from what the masses are doing. Even if it looks like fun, there's just something about it that turns me off when it's the popular thing to do. I told them I didn't want to do it, that I wanted to be different. I felt like everyone was writing a book, and I didn't want to be like everyone else. So, they politely backed off and left me to it.

About a year and a half later they came to me again, this time with "we have your second book for you." Again, I emphatically stated I didn't want to write a book, so they needed to figure out something else for me to do. And again, they backed off. The day came, about a year later when they stepped forward and, yup, you guessed it…they had my third book!

Now this was getting ridiculous. I asked them to explain what the deal was. They said, "You can deny our guidance but that doesn't mean your path leads anywhere else. This is your trajectory." And then, I instantly understood. Remember the two-by-four? Yeah, this was one of those moments.

I have the right to choose any path, but that doesn't mean it's the way my soul wished to go. Suddenly, I understood the difference between being attached to what I wanted and what would serve the Highest Good.

In the grand scheme of things, human perception is but a mere fraction of the whole picture, and I was very attached to my version of the story. So, reluctantly and with great nervousness, I began writing this book. It's gone through so many wardrobe changes, concept designs, and content revisions that I've actually lost track of all the versions. It's taken me six years to finally feel ready to share the information that I believe will leave you nourished and fed.

The first version was very light and fluffy…and very safe! Not to say that it was wrong, only that I was just scratching the surface of who I was to become. It wasn't until my practice shifted, and I began teaching shadow work that it really started to dig in and have some meat. That is what this latest version reflects. The depth. The nutrition.

The deliciousness that is life. The struggle. The pain. The growth. And expansiveness of it all. The point of the whole dang thing.

What Motivates Humans

I find it completely beautiful how every single human on the planet is having their own unique experience, while simultaneously playing with all the other humans that are having theirs. And then, taking it a step further, how intricately we all weave together in a perfect tapestry of life, love, and loss. It truly is what motivates me to do what I do. I love the perfection of it all. From the smallest, seemingly insignificant intersections to the biggest, most extravagant, life altering collisions, it inspires me to find out why we humans do what we do. Even though each of us is unique and individual, there are two things that bind us together and make us the same at the core.

(1) We are all seeking love and acceptance

(2) We all want to make our mark in the world

These two elements are our common denominators, the ties that bind you could say. They are the motivators for just about every decision we'll ever make in life. Regardless of the direction we go, all humans are driven by the same internal fire: to be loved and accepted and to be remembered and honored by their peers.

What's cool about those two points of passion is that they each nurture one half of our totality. The drive to make our mark in the world, to leave a legacy of our existence is the human/ego side of us. It is where our value as a human is based on the evidence that we existed. When we are remembered, we matter. The human ego is that part within us that craves to be special. It requires the experience of separatism. And it is extremely motivated to prove that "I" am a single unit in a vast sea of the whole. It drives our will and tantalizes that part of us that is competitive and wants to be important. Which is why so much of our day is spent comparing and judging ourselves and others.

The other half of our motivation is in seeking oneness with all that is. This is our spiritual side, or soul state. As we search to be loved and accepted as an individual, it is the part of us that somehow knows we are but a sliver of the wholeness that is Source energy. (Or you can call it whatever you want, God, Universe, and on and on.) Where our ego wants to be the one and only, our soul seeks the collective. And this is the whole experience in its most perfect expression of contrast. We run around the planet, bumping into one another, causing chain reactions that allow each person his or her own experience while simultaneously connecting each of us in a Divine Tapestry. And it is precisely that relationship between oneness and individualism that sets us up for the most brilliant of adventures.

Yes, life can throw curve balls, asteroids, and loop-to-loops. And sometimes we throw fits and hold our breath until we turn purple. And yet there are moments when we stand up, shake our fist at the sky and dare to ask for more. It's what makes it all so delicious. It's all about the experience of living life. It is entirely about having the contrast of going for it, getting dirty, falling down, picking ourselves back up again and figuring it out along the way. It's when we fall down that we really get clear on what it is we truly want.

And even though we are all so different, there is much that is the same. We are all thinking/feeling creatures, filled with a spiritual essence housed in a physical vehicle. And that "spirited vehicle" requires a little maintenance from time to time to function at its best. We may all drive different cars, but they are cars, nonetheless.

Whatever your religion or spiritual practice is, and/or your philosophy about life is in general, the tools within this book are simple enough to incorporate into your day-to-day routine and yet can have a profound impact on your overall disposition. Are they spiritual practices? Yes, they can be. Do you have to be spiritual to do them? Nope, not one bit. As we journey together, I'll try to use a variety of terms and jargon. I'll work on being in the middle of "woo-woo" and "science-y." We'll walk between the worlds of space cadets and pragmatists! And because my brain functions fluidly when I step-by-step my growth process, that is how we'll walk through this book. One baby step at a time. In fact, one of my very favorite quotes is by Creighton Williams Abrams, Jr., "When eating an elephant, take one bite at a time."

It's designed to be bite-sized breadcrumbs of tasty morsels smothered in a yummy sauce. One building on the other, allowing full integration and upgrades in awareness. Play with it. Have fun. Be open and willing. Take what feels good to you and throw away the rest. No one path works for us all. We must discover what resonates with each of us. I'm simply offering what has worked for me and my clients over the years. I hope they resonate with you as well.

So here we go, fork in hand, napkin on lap.

Let's dig in!

CHAPTER 1

Aware

One hundred percent of this book will never make a single bit of difference if we don't first talk about the *Art of Awareness*. It is the foundation on which everything else will be built going forward. The premise is quite simple really: if you aren't present to what you're doing, how you feel about it, and what you think about it, how can you make choices that support your Highest Good? You can't. You won't. If you are not aware of what you're doing, you'll almost always rely on habits, old programs, and knee-jerk response mechanisms. When we mindlessly march through life, we base our decisions on comfort, safety, and acceptance.

Now that might sound like a perfectly reasonable way to live, but it's not always the case. When you base your decisions on being comfortable, you'll rarely grow beyond your comfort zone. That's why it's called a comfort zone…you don't leave it to explore what else could be possible because it's just too uncomfortable. That can lead to living a very small life where fear is the dominating emotion. Basically if you think life is dangerous, you will want safety, shrinking your energy to become a smaller target for the perceived danger you think is out in the world. A small target is hard to hit, so instinctively we'll shrink in order to survive. Then, just to round off the recipe for "Living a Small Life," we add a dollop of covering up the wounds, a sprinkle of hiding the icky parts, and a splash of ignoring what's really under the surface. It can feel like our life is crashing down around us even though we're working really hard to keep our head above water. And anytime life gets too hard to face, we'll throw whatever has been wounded into the basement with the rest of the "garbage." That way we don't have to see it and be reminded of the pain.

But let's face it. Feeling those icky things pushing us out of our comfort zone truly helps us grow beyond what we've always had. Like a baby bird we get pushed out of the nest where we must learn very quickly how to fly. And thank goodness for that or our wings would eventually be useless!

Story Time

Perhaps it would help if we illustrated this point with a story: Meet Mike. Mike is an average guy, living life and trying to do his best. Only his best is dominated by stressing out, living in fear, and trying like hell to just survive. His perception of the world is that it's a dangerous place. This has his fight-or-flight response super heightened, ready for anything that might attack. And that's great on one level. We should be aware of our surroundings. But there is a difference between what we perceive as danger and what is truly harmful. When most of our focus is survival-based, our perception will judge anything uncomfortable as dangerous and something that should be avoided at all costs.

Because Mike's emotions run high with fear and worry, this leads him to choose experiences and relationships that will keep him within a certain level of comfort. He gravitates to things that feel familiar because there is some level of control in that situation. Even if that means the situation he is choosing is actually one that harms him. The need for familiarity offers a sense of comfort because at least he can count on it. This behavior is seen in situations where victims stay with their abusers. It hurts them, but it's comforting to know the pattern of abuse.

In order for Mike to stay in those not-so-great situations, he must create a certain level of denial and lack of responsibility for his choices. This keeps him away from the realization that he is the one sabotaging his own life. It's too difficult at that point for Mike to own up to the fact that he is the one perpetuating his circumstances. He buries it deep inside to keep that truth hidden so he can stay in his perceived comfort.

This act of protecting himself from having accountability begins to set Mike up for making other low risk decisions. He won't rock the boat for fear of unveiling the things he is hiding away. His life moves towards choices that are easy, non-threatening, and manageable. There is no great risk when living a small life.

The issue though is that some of the higher risk options are the very ones that could take him out of his fear and worry and catapult him into a life where he can thrive. Maybe he really needs to stretch his wings and try new adventures. That "something new" could have been a possible love connection or an offer to work at his dream job. It could have been an amazing new opportunity that would have really propelled his sense of purpose in the world, allowing him to feel joy and true connection with others.

But Mike's ego perceives these risks as dangerous, talks himself out of doing them, and settles back into his comfort zone. He's missed out on something amazing. And deep down inside, he knows it. He might try to ignore it, but he knows he played it safe. Every human has within them a Divine Wisdom, a voice inside that speaks the truth. Something deep within, Mike knows he sold out for safety.

As time goes by, that voice is nagging at him, reminding him that he's denying his greatness. If he decides to move towards taking ownership of his situation the nagging feeling will lessen. But if Mike chooses to ignore that voice, he'll begin to feel regret, disappointment, even anger. When he feels these emotions bubbling up, it's precisely what he didn't want to have happen. The boat begins to rock! He starts to panic because he's afraid that all that he's been hiding is about to reach the surface.

Rather than take responsibility, he'll project those emotions onto others. His current relationships will suffer further because he is blasting his emotions onto anyone within 50 feet of him.

In the meantime, he works feverishly to justify why he chose to stay put. He'll make up stories about why the bigger option was a stupid idea. Possibly even tearing himself down, saying he was never going to be good at it anyway. At this point, he'll say anything to validate why it was the better choice to stay in his comfort zone.

To stave off the continuing regret that he didn't listen to his internal truth, Mike gravitates towards something that will offer more comfort (sex, alcohol, food, drugs, etc.). It distracts and numbs him from taking any responsibility for his own life. This temporary fix mutes the Divine Wisdom, allowing him to stay in the ignorance-is-bliss phase.

Now from here, we can only expect things to go downhill for our guy. He might adopt a victim- or martyr-type personality trait. Codependent urges and addictive behaviors manifest, perpetuating a deeper lack of awareness. This leaves Mike feeling completely defeated, without the possibility of bouncing back. Each new thing that comes along will only push his buttons and spark more fear, causing him to shrink even smaller. All because that one opportunity looked too dangerous to risk.

As you can see in this downtrodden story, UN-awareness leads to more unawareness. Anytime we choose denial and numbness, it snowballs into bigger issues, setting us up for lifelong patterns. It may provide a temporary comfort but is it really and truly comfortable? No! A very hearty and resounding NO! It's completely fake comfort. False security fueled by justifications and rationalizations. It keeps us in a state of mindlessness and perpetuates a lack of responsibility for our choices. There is ZERO freedom in that way of life.

Are you wondering why Mike doesn't just change his mind and make a different choice? If he's really that unhappy, why doesn't he just take a risk and try something new?

There are so many reasons why we humans do what we do. Sometimes, it's just too difficult to face the patterns we have created. Having accountability for the circumstances of our lives can be incredibly challenging. Not to mention the huge amount of changes we'll have to make because we finally see the patterns. It can be terribly overwhelming. Remember, every person is unique in their own life experiences. We can't possibly know what has happened in someone's past that has them seeking that level of false comfort.

One thing is certain; like Mike, the story we tell is the key to unlocking the prison we have put ourselves in. It's the story we tell ourselves over and over again about why the world is dangerous and why we should stay inside to be safe. That story is the poisonous monster that keeps us small. We feed it with our fears and excuse it with our justifications while numbing it with our addictive choices. The story requires us to behave, to stay in line, and to not rock the boat. It needs order and submission from us. And in return, the story will keep feeding false comfort and doling out denial by the truckloads.

Once Upon a Time…

The human's ability to tell stories was once a sacred act. At one time it was a part of our tribal culture to pass down information from the elders to the younger generations. We sat around fires, sang our songs, and danced our sacred dances to tell the stories of our people. We taught our children with stories. We created our faithful practices and ritualistic lore from stories. In ancient times, storytelling was rich with nutrition that fed our community and carried us through the changing seasons.

In modern times we have abandoned the supportive nature of stories and twisted them to feed our ego selves. We cultivate these repetitive programs so that we can hide from the things that frighten us. As we tell them over and over, we begin to believe them. This perpetuates a sense of denial as we give ourselves permission to not take responsibility for our circumstances in life. But be not mistaken, the story is always the key. It's an eye-opening glimpse into why we might be struggling in life. That story can either make us or break us. We can either pump it full of life, allowing it to be the big monster under our bed, OR we can rip the blankets back, face it, and call it for what it is.

Growing up in my household was an interesting journey through minefields and emotional falsities. My mother was the Queen of Guilt Trips and the Master of Manipulation. And she taught her children well, passing the baton on to us by implanting those tendencies within each us. Over and over again, in subliminal body language, snide comments, and insulting accusations, she got the message across to me that I was worthless. No, she never actually said those words to me. But as we all know, communication isn't always just the words coming out of our mouths. I didn't even realize that her message had programmed within me so deeply until much further down the road.

Stories are tricky like that. We aren't aware of the harm they cause because we have gotten so used to hearing them over time. The repetitive stories become part of our everyday vernacular. Like a Trojan horse, they enter through our broken heart and settle in like a silent virus. That virus sits, festering and waiting for the moment it can proudly hit the repeat button on the tape recorder, playing the voice of the antagonist of our childhood over and over again.

As I grew into a young woman, I had a subconscious sense that I just wasn't worthy of love, friendship, abundance, joy, whatever…the list goes on. At that point in my life, I definitely was living to stay safe and driven subconsciously to simply have acceptance. Thanks to my mom's tutelage, I maneuvered the playing field with dexterity and cunningness. Manipulation was my best skill and I exercised it quite often, I'm afraid. I knew how to survive in the world. I knew when to play small. And I knew when to make excuses for my mistakes. I can even remember my go-to response. In the wake of my screw-ups, I would say, "It isn't my fault. My mother didn't give me very good tools."

Regardless how many times I blamed her, I would always seem to end up in the same place, sad and alone. I had no idea there was a negating belief within me that played like a broken record. I had no clue it was the one in control of my life. And it steered me into situation after situation, intently focused on the goal of not being hurt and staying safe. Which might sound like something we want, but truly it's the heart of the saboteur.

Looking back, I can see how many people I hurt because of this programming. Anytime "shit got real," I would bolt. I couldn't handle real. I had never had that and inside I didn't feel worthy of it. So in and out, years upon years, I played the game of wanting connection but being afraid of it and sabotaging any efforts to actually have it. Until I learned of this thing called a core story. Deep within me, a drum was beating the same message, playing into my subconscious, a story that I adopted from my mother. I am worthless. I am worthless. I am worthless.

When I realized it was there, it crushed me. At first, there was a small part of me that believed it had to be true. That was the reason for all of my heartache in life. I just simply wasn't worthy of being loved. It depressed me to the point of thinking of suicide. If I wasn't worth love, then I didn't deserve life. Everything started making sense

7

now as I reviewed my life up to that point. I justified, excused, and blamed other people. It was my mom's fault. It was my estranged father's fault. And it was my stepdad's fault. I blamed everyone I could think and yet took zero responsibility for my own actions. And I took it to the deepest, darkest part of my soul. I wallowed in my victimhood that the world had done me wrong. (Funny, now that I think about it, it's exactly how my mother would be reacting to this conversation.)

As time went on, I sought therapy, read books on the subject, and started to realize the power of storytelling. It was just something someone once said…but the power was in the fact that I agreed with them and adopted the story as my own. People say things about us all the time. It's not until we believe the possibility that story might be true that their story has power over us. So if I believed it, then that meant I could also UN-believe it now and create a story that supported me.

My logical mind started seeing how there is no way I was worthless. Of course I had worth. I may have not known what it was at that point but I could sure try and find out. Out of the hole I began to climb. I realized it was a choice to believe in the story and if I didn't like the particular one I was telling, I could simply change my mind and focus on one I liked. It's all just words, mixed with emotions and thoughts anyway, right? Nothing is ever really true until you believe it to be so.

Please don't get me wrong. It was tough to catch that little bugger! It popped up in the darnedest of places, seeking to put me back in the corner and regain control over my life. In fact, it took a lot of energy to stay on top of it. I had to watch for those moments when it would whisper in my ear that I was worthless. And when (or if) I caught it, I would have to talk it down and remind myself that I did deserve good things in my life. In the beginning, it was a tiresome battle. But eventually, I got better at catching it, and the whispering grew faint and before I knew it, I started believing – and better yet – living as if I had value!

Who You Gonna Call?

One of my favorite movie examples for this topic is a scene in *Ghostbusters 2*. The pivotal point of the movie's plot is when Ray, Winston, and Egon are in the old tunnels under New York City and there they find a river of slime. They all end up in the slime and eventually climb out of a manhole onto the street level. Once everyone is out and safe, they begin to argue, almost to the point of fighting each other. Egon realizes it's the slime making them act that way and instructs them to quickly remove their outer suits. Once they do, they instantly feel back to normal. They explain in the movie that the slime is the source of all the anger and hatred that New Yorkers express, only no one knows it's there. They just act out without paying attention to why they are so angry all the time.

The reason this is such a great parable for shadow work is that it perfectly illustrates the core story idea. The river of slime is our core story. It's deep within us, underneath the surface in our subconscious. We don't know it's there and yet, it affects our behavior. Whatever the story, it has a hold on us. It constantly whispers that you can't, you shouldn't, and you aren't able. On whatever level it speaks to you - trust me - it does a lot of talking! Until we can dig deep enough and uncover what the story is saying, it will always be in control of our lives.

The Princess and the Pea

Another way of looking at it is by using the old fairytale of *The Princess and the Pea*. My Guys always use this story to take this conversation just a bit further. It's much the same as we remember, but they have put their spin on the moral of the story.

Their version goes like this: The princess wants to sleep but she can't get comfortable enough to rest because something is digging into her back. She keeps adding mattresses in the hopes that she will finally be comfortable enough to sleep. But to no avail. Finally, she rips back the mattresses, one by one, only to discover at the very bottom of the pile is a pea. A single, tiny pea. Something you wouldn't think would cause that much discomfort, especially with all the mattresses to cushion her from it. It's only when she decides to investigate the situation, digging down deep until she finds it, can she finally rest.

Our core story is the same as that pea. Oh it's there! Digging into our psyche and manipulating our subconscious, making it impossible to relax and rest, keeping us from being happy and hijacking our inner value to negate our dreams and goals. And we try so hard to cover it up, stacking up mattress after mattress in the hopes that we'll finally be able to ignore it. The mattresses represent our false comforts and diversion tactics. We try like hell to numb the pain and ignore the truth, but it's there. And until we dig down, rip off the false comforts, and expose the kernel for what it is, it will never let us truly rest.

Just the Facts, Ma'am

Remember that old television show, *Dragnet?* Whenever I get into this topic about core stories with my clients, my Guys always say, "Just the facts, ma'am." It makes me laugh every time, but they're so right. We don't need to be spinning tales of perception, excuses, and justifications. We've got no time to weave our webs of illusion and storytelling. Let's just stick to the facts.

Aware

I learned years ago that there are three things that happen when we experience any type of event in our life.

- First, we simply experience it. We have it, in all its glory, for all it's worth. It happened. Whether we planned it or it came by surprise and regardless if we enjoyed it or not. That's life! A hustling bustling bombardment of happenings.

- Second, we react to the event. It's simple cause and effect really. It happens. We react. If it's a pleasant experience, we react in a blissful, joyous kind of way. If it's hurtful, we react by recoiling and defending ourselves.

- Third, we interpret what just happened based on our reaction to it. We begin telling our stories, projecting feelings and judgments, and speculating about how we perceive others acted. The story begins to grow, right there, in the interpretation. We place judgments on the people involved and carry out the sentence depending on how it made us feel. If we liked it, we celebrate. If we didn't, we condemn. We rarely consider our responsibility in it because we are too busy living in the reaction, interpretation, and storytelling.

Our powers of storytelling are so strong that we allow them to steer our course, drive our decisions, and justify ending relationships. Regardless if what we believed happened is actually what happened. This is the true reactionary human, jumping to conclusions based on perception. Our stories become wildfires. Blame and defensiveness provide the necessary fuel, which grows the flames even higher and hotter, until finally, they consume us.

We don't really focus on the facts. We revel in the story. And we share it with others, retelling our version of the events and how it affected us. We lobby to gain their vote for who is to blame and why we are justified in being the victim. We tell it, and tell it, and tell it again.

11

Fueling it with emotions and judgments, until the story isn't anywhere near the actual event. It's snowballed and grown beyond recognition. It now breathes on its own and has its own life force, increasing in strength each time the story is shared.

This type of behavior can get us off track in life. We are but our perceptions, or in this case, our interpretations. And our interpretations eventually become our reality. The more we tell the story, the more we (and others) begin to believe it. The more we believe it, the more we begin to change our behavior towards those people. One misunderstanding can have a ripple effect that could change the course of our whole life.

Right or Happy?

When we experience a negative event, the first thing we tend to do is to place a story around it. We tell these stories not just to communicate what happened but to express how it made us feel and what it did to us. We lobby others for sympathy and validation, hoping to grow our numbers and gain followers. We're looking for those who will corroborate the story that we have been done wrong by the antagonist of that moment. With every "vote," we are vindicated. The more and more we tell this tale, the more we breathe life into it. The stories begin to program us with a new illusion of reality. Fueling that fire is the drive to be right. Our fragile ego just isn't in the game to be wrong and it will fight to the end to prove it is the victor. Even if that means winning a game that is hurting us.

Over time, as we retell our stories again and again, we eventually merge with our stories. They become the programming for our subconscious computer. We start living from that new "reality," changing our behaviors and steering our decisions because of them. Eventually, we draw towards us a new experience from that old story.

12

The program comes to life, actualizing right before our eyes, making it possible for us to proudly exclaim "See, I told you so!"

Let's give an example. Let's say a young lady named Lucy has been in a relationship where her partner was unfaithful. This created a story that "everyone cheats." Harboring the unresolved, painful memories, she reluctantly goes into a new relationship with a guy named Jake, fearing he will follow suit. Lucy tries to drown out the subconscious fear, but the drum beats on. With rhythmic precision, her story grows stronger. It whispers in Lucy's ear, "I know he is going to cheat because everyone cheats." Before she knows it, the story overcomes logic and reason and she succumbs to it.

Paranoia gets the better of her and she begins to spy on Jake, checking his phone and email, even going so far as to accuse him of infidelity without proof. Sadly, let's say that Jake does commit the crime. Now, Lucy can say she was right. But did he do it on his own volition, or did Lucy subliminally implant the thought and he acted on it?

Who's to say, really? I could talk about how Lucy possibly picked the person that would cheat on her because she was familiar with that trait. Even though it was an unwanted experience, she feels more comfortable with that outcome and knows what to expect. Or maybe on a subconscious level, she wanted to further claim that she was indeed a victim. By allowing another relationship to end in the same manner, she can gain sympathy and support from her friends and family. This is typically the behavior of someone who is addicted to being the victim.

Whatever the reason, Lucy continues to attract the same kind of partner. We all do. At least, until we figure out how to heal what is out of balance within ourselves. There is strong evidence that we subconsciously choose these relationships. Haven't you ever had the same experience over and over, but with different people? This is the pattern our stories perpetuate.

According to relationship psychologist Harville Hendrix, we tend to attract the mates that have the positive and negative traits of our caregivers. He coined the term Imago, which is Latin for "image" and refers to the "unconscious image of familiar love." In his book, *Getting the Love You Want*, Hendrix explains that we always choose a partner that mirrors the places in us that we need to develop in ourselves. This is why when we first meet someone we love everything about them. But a little down the road we'll be frustrated with the very traits we first admired in them.

Every single interaction with another human holds valuable nutrition that can show us the wounds that lie deep within. All that is occurring on the surface isn't the real issue. We draw these things in to alert us that something is wounded deep down. This is why we tend to have patterns in our life. It isn't that we are dumb and just keep walking into the brick wall. It's that the brick wall has a deeper message. It's up to us to be willing to look past what's in front of us and into the deeper meaning.

A Pondering: I personally believe that humans are master creators and that we constantly attract situations to give us the opportunity to heal what is wounded. I think this because, as I've said, my original story stated, "I am worthless." On top of that I had a secondary story that stated, "Everyone cheats." And wouldn't you just know it, I attracted a varying array of cheaters that would agree to my lack of worth. I got a double scoop of crap. It didn't matter how many different types of people I dated, the story would show up the same way every time. I was picking the wrong kind of guy because of these two programs. Not to punish myself, but to give myself the

opportunity to dig down through the garbage and find the wounds
these stories originated from.

The clincher was when I realized each guy had traits that my mother
had. Bingo! I was dating my mom! Gross! Now that the pattern was
uncovered, I knew it was up to me to heal what was broken. I dug in
deep, faced my fears, and acknowledged my wounds. I had to face
things that I wanted to hide from. I had memories of events I didn't
know existed. Like a plumber snaking a drain, the gook and grime
bubbled up to the surface. And it wasn't pretty. I mourned. I cried. I
let myself be angry. I gave myself whatever I felt I needed in that
moment in support of my process.

After a little while, I started to feel lighter. I saw my relationships
shift. New people came into my life, and they saw my worth (even if
I wasn't quite there yet). Little by little, I started telling myself a new
story. A story that speaks about how I deserved to be cherished, that
I am worthy of being loved. Doing so allowed me to be open to
choosing a different kind of person to be in my life, and I am now
happy to say that I am truly loved and valued.

Whatever the reason our Lucy chose her path to take, the fact
remains that she now has another valid piece of evidence that proves
everyone cheats. Therefore, her story strengthens. So the dominating
belief created her reality. And when we can count on a story playing
out systematically, we have a certain level of control over it. We may
hate that it happens but we know how to behave when it does. We'll
favor what is familiar over the unknown risk of letting the story die
away.

Now, why would we do this? You would think that we would
rather be happy than to manifest another negative experience in our

lives. But, oddly enough, it seems we would rather be right than happy. To do that, we tell stories over and over until they actualize. Now, we are able to claim not only that we are right but we also feed the story that we are victims and it wasn't our fault. But, here's a little tip...we manifested the whole dang thing! By telling the story over and over, we claimed that experience and demanded we be right about it. And guess what. It worked! The more you beat the drum of your story, the more you will experience it in your life. It's unavoidable! That's how powerful we are! We are creation beings and are keenly skilled in the art of drawing into our experience the events that we call forth. Even the ones that suck!

The Point of Paying Attention

As we move forward let me again say: Without the ability to be self-aware, you will more than likely make choices that do not fully support you. We must work to move away from the denial and victimhood and towards being proactive and owning our part in the experience. We can only do this by being in the state of awareness.

One of my earliest awarenesses of, well awareness, was while living in Tucson, Arizona. A friend and I were sitting on her back patio, chilling with some wine and talking about the mysteries of the Universe. We had spent some time that night theorizing and philosophizing about life, the afterlife, and all of the deliciousness in between. Then suddenly, one of us - I can't remember who now - said something pretty catty. We went from a high vibrational conversation to the average gossip in a hair salon. And instantly, there was a drop in vibration so palpable that I felt it deep in my gut area. It was as if I were on a rollercoaster that had just topped the first free fall drop. It was out of place enough to grab our attention. We both looked at each other in shock and decided we would test it out further.

So we got back to our mind-expanding, positive conversation, and then purposely slipped into gossip once more. Without missing a beat, there it was again, the icky sludge. And my tummy was telling me all about it. My body was giving me the indicator that it wasn't okay with the change in topic and was supporting me to stay in the high vibrational area. What a concept!

Excited to understand more I took it upon myself to continue this experiment. I handled my day-to-day tasks like always but focusing a little attention on my tummy. As I listened to people talk, I would check in with my gut area to see what it might be telling me. I specifically watched for the "rollercoaster" moment when it would drop. If I caught it, I would try to figure out what made it do that.

As I progressed, I started seeing how certain people's words would affect me emotionally as well as physically. This allowed me to also practice my boundaries by not feeding into their conversations. It was so much fun, and to this day, I credit my love for clean communication to this very first "game." (My Guys call them games because they want to keep it fun. And they think they're gameshow hosts. So adorable!) I love to support my tummy, and she demands I talk with intention. It truly was the moment that birthed this entire journey for me. That is why I start here, with this book, with this chapter. The Art of Awareness. It is everything!

How can you change anything if you aren't aware you don't like it? So, I lovingly challenge you to go out into the world and play your own awareness game. Listen to your words, pay attention to your body. Focus on what others are saying and recognize how your body reacts. Simply observe and mentally take notes. When you start seeing the patterns you are now deciphering your body's language. It *is* talking to you. Are you listening?

CHAPTER 2

Anchor

First things first! We need a strong foundation. When an architect begins a project, much of the focus is put towards securing the structure so that it stands the test of time. Sculptors and other artists take the same first steps when birthing their creative projects. They must take into account the weight, proportion, and positioning of their artworks to make sure that they will remain in place and not fall over crushing someone to death. Anyone who has ever erected a larger-than-life project knows it needs sure footing and a strong anchor.

Human beings aren't much different when you think about it. We tend to do better in our endeavors when we have a solid ground to walk on. Our eyes align with the horizon, the tiny hairs in our inner ears balance us when we stand up, and our muscles stabilize us as we move about. We feel our best when we're clear, focused, and sure of our surroundings. It allows for a more proactive sense of existence rather than a reactive state of survival.

Where We Are in Space

One of my very favorite words in the whole English language is proprioception. According to Wikipedia:

Proprioception: (/ˌproʊpri.əˈsɛpʃən/ PRO-pree-o-SEP-shən), from Latin proprius, meaning "one's own," "individual," and perception, is the sense of the relative position of neighbouring parts of the body and strength of effort being employed in movement.

In my thirties, I worked as a personal trainer. We used this word to explain why, when standing on one foot, the ankle and leg shake. Signals to the brain indicate a possible loss of balance. The brain then alerts the muscles in the leg to stabilize the body. Short muscle fibers begin to fire back and forth, pushing the ankle, calf, and knee left and right to keep the human from falling. The muscles make tiny, microsecond adjustments, which appear to us as being shaky. They are working extra hard to maintain the balance for the whole body by reading where it is in relation to its surroundings and horizon line.

If we take this concept internally and think about how that affects our awareness, we can see the importance of proprioception in our daily navigation. Much like the inner ear and muscle fibers, our thoughts, emotions, and overall disposition can signal that we are either headed in a direction that works for us or it can sound the alarm that we are barreling towards danger. Checking in with our internal indicators provides clearer navigation and allows us to see the horizon line once again.

Navigating this vast and crazy game called *Life* can be tricky. With all of the demands put upon us, the different roles we have to play, and the never-ending laundry that seems to magickally pile up, it's no wonder we lose our way sometimes. When we are flailing in life and feeling discombobulated, our horizon line is fuzzy and our sense of "where we are in space" gets lost. In those moments, it seems like nothing is working and we can't quite get our head above water. Thank goodness, there is something we can do about it.

Grounding

The process of grounding is the act of connecting to that anchor. It is a proactive tool that links us with the planetary energy that is so beautifully available to us all. Much like when you go camping, the first thing you might do is put up your tent. If you do so without staking it down, guess what happens when the tiniest of breezes blows by? It will fall and tumble away. But when you hammer in those stakes, secure the straps and anchor it, you stand a better chance at staying sheltered for the night, regardless of the weather. We humans are much like tents. We need an anchor to help us stand strong when the winds howl.

Let's look at it another way. Pretend that you are a beautiful, red helium balloon. Without a string tying you down you will go wherever the four winds blow and you have no say in the matter. But if you tie yourself to something heavy, like a rock, you may dance and dart in the wind but you have the connection to something substantial and you stay put. It isn't a confinement. It is an anchor. A touchstone to reset your proprioception.

Ocean Waves

Let's drive this home from another angle. Imagine yourself in the ocean. The water is about waist high and your feet are firmly planted on the sandy bottom. You can feel the slight push and pull of the rhythmic tide as your toes try to grip the sand for balance. Noticing that the ebb and flow is getting stronger, you widen your stance to give yourself a stronger base. Just when you think you're secure a large wave swallows you up and forces you under water. Try as you may to stay upright, eventually it tumbles you to shore.

But now visualize your legs buried in the sand up to your knees and the water is again at your waist. The push and pull is still prevalent and the waves come like clockwork, but now you have a bit of leverage to keep yourself upright. Your strong legs are firmly planted, providing you with the perfect foothold. The waves may crash and knock you down, but you pop right back up.

I use this metaphor with my clients to explain to them that life is much like this. We experience many waves of change, breakdown, growth, and pain. Waves come and wipe us out, but they also wash away what no longer needs to be there. We don't always know when they are coming and often times, find ourselves tumbling under the water gasping for air. We can't do anything about the waves of change. They are one of the constants in life.

By being proactive and utilizing tools such as grounding, we stand a better chance at remaining strong and secure as the waves crash around us. Being grounded gives us something to grab onto when life would normally knock us down. Our eyes are fixed on the horizon, and we have clarity for the journey ahead. Sometimes, that can make all the difference in our world.

Breaking it Down

So what exactly *is* grounding? It's the act of connecting your energy with the energy of the planet. Sound simple? It is. Amazingly so. So much, in fact, that we wonder why we should even do it. Since humans generally run on the program "No Pain, No Gain" we tend to not trust things that come easily. We seem to equate things that are easy to having a lower value while simultaneously believing that if it is difficult it must be important. Trust me when I say, it's the easiest thing to do and the most valuable technique you could practice.

Okay, so if that's *what* it is, then *how* is it done? Through visualization, meditation, or simply by saying it is so and holding the conviction that you are grounded is the *how*. I know, this is where it might get a bit sticky and many of you are preparing to scoff in my general direction. So without getting overly woo-woo, let's walk through the steps of one way to ground yourself. I recommend grounding every day, preferably in the mornings before heading off to what awaits you.

First, the basics:

1. When just starting out, I recommend you give yourself plenty of time and someplace quiet where you can focus. Try to not put any time constraints on this exercise. Add it to your morning routine of meditation. Or sit quietly in a chair, on the floor, or under your favorite tree. As you get more experienced you will be able to ground even in the noisiest of malls with a million kids screaming for the latest video game. (Trust me. I've done that!)

2. The key is to relax and not push the process. Overthinking, judging you're doing it wrong, and forcing it will only frustrate you. So start by closing your eyes and taking a couple of slow, deep breaths. When you exhale allow your body to sink into itself a bit deeper, relaxing yet remaining alert. Take your awareness to your body, your breath, your posture, etc. Make any adjustments for your comfort. Let go of the outside world for just a bit. It'll be there when you're done. Don't worry. For now, just focus on you.

3. Next take your attention to the area of your body where your tailbone sits. This is where the root chakra is located. It's also the area of the body that grounding directly affects (more on chakras later). This is the part of the game where whatever you choose to visualize is up to you. But to keep it easy, let's just imagine your spine starting to grow down into the Earth, fanning out much like a tree's root system would. You might even imagine that you are a tree, your body being the trunk and your arms are the limbs growing towards the sky. But keep your focus for now on the roots. Allow them to spread out into the planet, going deeper and deeper until reaching the center of the Earth.

4. For a brief moment, sit and be present with what you've done. Just as a tree would, begin to drink in the nourishing energies that the planet has to offer. Drink in through the roots, drawing it back up towards your tailbone area and simply allow the energy to pool up in the root chakra. Don't worry about visualizing the actual chakra if you aren't comfortable with it. Just draw the energy up into that space and know it's feeding you. Be sure to give gratitude to the planet; that's always a nice thing to do.

5. After a few moments, open your eyes, recognize how you feel, and go about your day. If you find yourself needing to do it again, go for it. It never hurts to ground, regardless how many times a day you do it. Plus, the more you do it, the easier it gets. You can't OD on grounding! Have fun with it!

Side Note: So just in case you're thinking why is something so simple so important? The root chakra rules over how safe and secure we feel in our day to day lives. It is where our survival instinct is the greatest. When the root is fed by drinking in planetary energy, it feels open, anchored, and nourished. It feels strong and supported, creating a solid foundation. It *is* our proprioception...it lets us know where we are (and more specifically, how we're doing) in our space. When the root is unsupported, it tends to get sluggish and closes down to reserve its energy. Therefore, the safety/security alarm that resides in the root has us feel fearful and over-reactive to normally benign situations. So yeah, it's kind of a big deal.

Optional Grounding Techniques

If you're anything like me, and I think a few of you are, you tend to get bored doing the same ol' thing every day. You want variety! Yes! The spice of life! Visualizing you're a tree is great, but after you've done it for a couple of months, it can get really old. And boring! And we humans tend to not do things when we are bored and uninspired. Ask anyone that has ever made any kind of New Year's resolution. We are always excited in the beginning but if we don't keep it fresh and fun, we aren't inspired to keep it up and will eventually stop.

So, in the spirit of keeping things fresh and varietal, let's talk about some fun grounding options. Remember, it's all about using your imagination. The actual technique doesn't matter. It's the end result we're going for. If you feel better after grounding, then you did it correctly. Remember that above all else.

Here are some of my favorites:

- **Tree:** This is always a great way to start due to the fact that most of us have seen one and can easily imagine its anatomy. As you sit and become relaxed, imagine your body as the trunk of a tree while your lower body is starting to reach into the Earth, sprouting roots in the dirt. Grow them down towards the center of the planet, and let them wrap around the metal core, letting that weight be your anchor. Hold that image for a few moments while you allow your roots to drink in the nutrition of Mother Earth. Draw it up into your trunk and let it nourish your tree.

- **Volcano:** Being a Fire Sign, I love this one. I imagine that my body *is* the volcano. I see the lava pooling up, under the Earth's crust, just below my physical body. I then channel it up through my root chakra and allow it to collect. My intention here is to use the fire energy to burn away any impurities in my system. I drink it into my root, allowing it to roll around like a brilliant fireball of healing energy. Then, I'll pull the lava up into my sacral chakra, roll it around, burning and purifying. One by one, I gather the fire into each chakra and allow it to do its job. Once it reaches the top of my head, I make it erupt like the magnificent volcano it is, letting the lava flow all around me. I use this visualization often when I'm feeling heavy and in need an energy lift. (Again, we'll cover the Chakra System in a later chapter.)

- **Geiser/Water Fountain:** Some people resonate more with water than fire. That works, too. You can do the same visualization, only this time use water in place of the lava. There are some days when I'm feeling emotionally sensitive and fire is just too much energy for me. So, water is the perfect choice as I hold the intention of it being cooling, soft, and fluid rather than hot and fiery.

- **Corkscrew:** There are times when I am so tired and stressed that grounding is all I have the energy for. Those are usually moments when I've not taken care of myself and have gotten so strung out with work that I'm a mess! So, I'll visualize myself sitting in lotus position on top of the planet and then see my tail bone turn to metal and begin to corkscrew into the Earth's crust, much like if you are opening a bottle of wine. I make it spiral out really wide, all the way to the center. In that moment I feel so secure that nothing will shake me. This simple act tends to bring my stress levels down allowing some much needed rest and recuperation.

- **Spaceship:** I was reading for a friend back in Boise and we figured out that she was an incarnated star person. Without getting too deep into that conversation, basically her home planet isn't Earth. Her soul hails from another star system and yet she wanted to see what it would be like to live as a human

26

this time around. Because of this, she found conventional grounding to be very difficult. Being that this isn't her home, the thought (and feeling) of anchoring here was a sense of repulsion to her spiritual/star side. And yet because she did decide to incarnate on Earth, her human side really needed that anchor for support. So, we came up with a unique visualization to satisfy her "human" while also giving her "star" the freedom of choice. We put her in a spaceship of her own design, sitting at the controls, looking out the window. She pushed a button on the console and dropped down a cable with a grappling hook. It would hook onto a metal connector which was securely bolted and anchored deep into the Earth's crust. Being in complete control of that process satisfied her need to be unattached, and yet gave her the feeling of being anchored and secure. Furthermore, since she was hovering above the planet in her spaceship it provided the sense of not completely being human. That exercise offered her the sensation of being connected to the strength of the planet but allowed her to remain unconfined and able to release the cable at any time, satisfying both sides of her being. We were both very pleased and excited for that insight. (This visualization won't resonate with everyone. But if it does and you aren't sure why, just go with it. Try it out and see how you can tailor it to make this one to be perfect for you.)

- **The Mother's Womb:** On the rare occasion, when I am emotionally raw and tender, it's difficult for me to be "in action" for myself. I crave the quietness and safety of the dark. While lying in bed in the fetal position under my comfy blankets, I'll visualize myself sinking into the center of the planet and being like a baby resting in the womb of Mother Earth. My intention here is to do nothing. Simply rest and be quiet while feeling the Divine Mother connection. It feeds my heart and soul and gives me permission to just stop for a moment and rest. Something I think we're all guilty of not doing enough.

- **When All Else Fails:** What happens when you try everything you know and you just can't seem to get it? Be patient and keep practicing. It takes time to learn new processes after a lifetime of doing something a certain way. And it takes even more time to trust ourselves in that process. We'll often wonder if we're doing it right and will question ourselves incessantly. Be gentle with yourself, keep practicing, and stay open to discovering how this process works for you. Don't worry about mastering this right away. Part of the skill is in being present to what it is, not forcing it to be what you think it should be.

These are all just jumping off points to get you started. Make up your own, have fun with them, and be inspired. And since it is all about intention and having an active imagination, you can't do it wrong. Remember, I always recommend having more than one way to ground. It keeps it fresh and alive. If it gets stagnant and boring, that's when we're more apt to stop doing it. So, get in there and be creative! Let your imagination explore and be free!

And what's great is the more you practice any new skill, the easier it gets over time. I liken it to syphoning gas from a car. Sure in the beginning it takes a little effort and sometimes it sucks! (Ha-ha, get it?) But once you get the hang of it - and more truthfully, once the root feels stronger - it takes less effort and time to ground. The biggest hurdle I think for people is remembering to actually do it. You can set timers on your phone, put up some notes around your home or work area, or maybe have an accountability buddy to do it with you. That way you can share in the adventure and help keep each other on track.

Centering

Okay, by now your root chakra is grounded, connected to Mother Earth, and feeling juicy! It's happily feeding the human side of you and satisfying the need for security in a rather topsy-turvy world. Bonus! But that is only one half of the conversation entitled "Being a Kickass Human Being!"

We now get to focus on the other half of your makeup, your spiritual side. Now, before you get grumpy because you think we're about to jump off the deep end and get all "woo-woo," let me remind you that your body does house a spiritual essence. You could call it a Soul or Spirit. Most Eastern philosophies refer to it as chi or qi, which translates to mean "life force energy." Regardless what you label it, it is the essence that animates your meat suit. And in order for the soul to come to Earth and experience the full-meal-deal of being a human, your soul must travel within a physical vehicle. And the human body cannot survive without that spiritual essence. It's the perfect marriage between material and immaterial, and therefore the spiritual requires just as much attention as our physical. So, let's not jump onto the things-just-got-weird bandwagon yet.

The Known Universe

The act of centering is much like grounding in that it is entirely intentional and it is all about connection and anchoring. However, centering is where you meld your spirit with Universal Energy rather than staking your human essence to a physical planet. This process nourishes the crown chakra, which is located at the top of your head and does so by connecting to the Universal Energy that exists in everything. It's just there. Everywhere. I personally call it The All, but it's known by many names such as Christ Consciousness, The Cosmos, Source and so on. The label doesn't really matter; that's a personal choice. Try not to get too hung up on what to call it and instead, work towards accepting that "It" is just there.

I read once that scientists have openly admitted that they have only been able to measure 4% of the Universe. In other words, everything that exists in this vastness of all that is, we only know 4% of it. That means that 96% is unanswered, undocumented, unknown, and cannot be measured by scientific means! They call it dark matter and dark energy. Not in the context to mean it is bad or evil but that it is not within our understanding. Therefore, it is in the dark. We have no clue! Every single thing we currently know is in that 4%. Pause if you will, and just let that sink in.

The crown chakra is our spiritual tether to that Universal Energy. It is our connection with The All. Without that partnership we are extremely reactionary, simple-minded humans, living in fear, running around making all of this stuff REAL! We invest way too deeply in our stories and our existence feels quite literally a life or death situation. We throw around judgments and criticism like they are beads at Mardi Gras. And when others throw them at us, we attack in defense. We believe people when they say we are worthless and we allow them to dictate what we should be in life.

Without the centering effect for our crown, we would really believe that these human games are the only point to life. It is in our connection to Source that allows us to be invested in the bigger picture. We know somewhere inside of us that this is a temporary stop along the journey. We live here, yes, but we don't have to buy into the story that our value means nothing beyond this physical existence.

Side Note: Please understand. This isn't me trying to convert anyone to a different belief system. I am convinced that we live multiple lives throughout this vast existence. But by no means am I requiring you to come along if you don't agree. Whatever you believe is perfect for you, and I honor that. Again - and I'll say it a million more times - simply take what is being offered as a possibility, keep what speaks to your soul, and throw away the rest. I am in no way an expert on all that exists within this vast realm. I simply believe in what I believe.

Gotta Have Faith

Our crown chakra provides a sense that there is something more than our mere mortality. It gives us faith. Faith in something bigger than just this little blue ball floating in space. And I'm not only talking about spiritual or religious faith. I'm talking about faith in ourselves, in our ability to thrive and achieve great things. It's about having faith in others, in love, in the beauty we put into the world. It is the fuel that moves this physical vehicle around from place to place. Without passion and drive, we're just, well, human. Living our lives, paying our bills, doing whatever we do day-to-day because that's what we're told to do to survive. When the crown chakra is open and connected we have a sense of purpose. We are driven to be a part of something bigger and to make it beautiful.

Optional Centering Techniques

As I spoke before about grounding and explained how to anchor your energy into the planet, I'm betting you had an easy time grasping that concept. Your brain was probably able to reach out and visualize my directions. We are, after all, on the planet. We have an excellent reference point to pull from. But if I were to say reach your mind up into the Cosmos and anchor your energy into that of the Universe, your brain may struggle a bit to formulate just how to do that. To reach up into the nothingness, to anchor into something invisible can be a more difficult concept to grasp. In our physical experience we tend to understand material over immaterial, thus leaving us a little lost when we speak of that realm. It's perfectly natural because we are physical creatures.

As we practice centering, it provides the opportunity to stretch our creative wings a bit and use our imaginations. So, this too is purely intentional and you can be as fancy as you want. Go for broke. Try a few different ways and zero in on your favorites.

Here are a few that I've tried and tested over the years:

- **Tree:** Go back to our first example of being a tree. Your body is the trunk and you've grounded your roots deep within the Earth. Now, imagine reaching up with your arms and sprouting limbs. Reach high into the sky, touching the light and drawing in sunshine. Imagine rain dropping down lightly on your leaves, quenching your thirst. The warm breeze blows through your limbs and swirling around you in a perfect dance. Feel the energy, channeling it through your branches. Draw it down into the top of your head, filling up your crown and aligning you to Source Energy. This is why the Celts use the Tree of Life symbol. It perfectly represents both Heaven and Earth connection, weaving them together as one.

- **Cables/Cords:** Let's say you chose to ground yourself by the use of a strong cable or cord, staked into the center of the Earth. See the same style of grounding cord, only this one is coming from the top of your head, reaching up and grabbing the Sun in the same manner. The grounding cable is anchoring you into the planet while the centering cable has you suspended below the Sun. Feel strong, connected, and perfectly fed. Draw the Sun's energy into your crown and let it nourish that part of you that craves Universal Energy.

- **Drain the Tub:** As you are sitting on top of the planet, imagine the swirling view of the galaxy above. Watch the stars and planets dance in a magnificent light show. With your intention, reach up and swirl the stars so that they begin to form a tornado-shaped cone. Much like how a bathtub drains in a whirlpool fashion, see the celestial bodies begin to funnel down towards the top of your head and pour inside of you. Allow all that the Cosmos has to offer, saturating you with galactic nutrition. Take it all the way down to your toes, as if you filling a glass up with milk. See every cell in your body drink in that light, feeling refreshed, nourished, and enlivened.

- **Figure 8:** A few years ago I had a client that was having difficulty both grounding and centering. When she came for her next session we decided to ask her HS what she needed. I was given the image of a figure eight that anchored her root chakra in the Earth and her crown chakra into the Sun. This particular technique may not work for everyone. If you have a fear of space, the darkness, or feeling alone/isolated, please tread lightly. The last thing we want is to induce a panic attack during a process that is intended to relax you. Due to there being a few moving parts with this one, let me give you a visual aid to support your journey. Begin by getting comfortable and allowing yourself this time to be present with yourself. You won't want to rush this process and yet the more you practice, the less time and effort it will take to complete it. As always, be gentle with yourself and try to not force it. In the illustrations that follow you will find a step-by-step explanation of this technique.

Anchor

Step 1: Visualize yourself floating peacefully in space, equidistant from the Sun and Earth. You are safe, you can breathe, and all is well. Remember, meditation is simply using your imagination. You can create anything that helps you relax deeper into this exercise.

Step 2: From the root chakra, take an energy cord through the center of the Earth and loop it back towards you. Perhaps visualize it as if you were taking a needle and threading it through a bead. Keep looping it around until the flow is self-sustaining. No need to rush or force it. Take your time, work with your own energy. The circuit is feeding your physical and nourishing the root.

Step 3: Once the root energy loop is moving on its own, take your focus to your crown chakra. Loop the same type of energy cord through the Sun (thread the bead again), this time using your crown chakra connection. Loop it back, knowing that it is nourishing everything in your spirit. And again, keep the flow going until it can do it on its own. For a few moments, simply be the observer of this exchange of energy.

Step 4: When you are ready, with intention connect the two loops in a figure 8, crossing at your center (heart chakra). Flowing down into the Earth, up into the Sun, and always passing through your heart. Over and over again, flowing and feeding all that you need. Create a figure eight of beautifully nourishing energy.

Houston, We Have a Problem

Troubleshooting is a huge part of staying in alignment as a human. Being able to determine that you are "not yourself" and then delving into your spiritual toolbox to find something that will assist you is what being aware and proactive is all about.

When we are not grounded or centered for a short period of time, we might notice small disturbances in our energy levels, mood, and mental state. If we continue to ignore that something feels off, these issues will increase, eventually manifesting bigger problems. Much like a clock would if some of the gears clicked out of alignment with the overall machine. When the cogs do not align, the entire contraption breaks down. One little slip of one single gear can wreak havoc for the whole design.

Fatigue, irritability, drastic mood swings, and even body aches and cold/flu symptoms are just some of the ways our complex design tries to get our attention. The genuineness of this alarm system is so the misaligned components can alert us that they are not doing well, thereby giving us the information to take action on their behalf. Our overall systems see that we are misaligned and disconnected from our center. The components are trying to protect the whole organism by making you aware of the misalignment.

You could call them symptoms, I suppose, but I like to see them as simple indicators of how we're doing in our experience. "Symptoms" to me lends to the feeling that someone is sick or dying and that can cause fear and stress hormones to pump through our bodies. And we don't need to create problems. We're looking for proactive solutions. Prolonged bouts of stress causes the over-production of Cortisol, which has been linked to several conditions and diseases. That brings the term "stress kills" to a whole new level.

Paying attention to our bodies, emotions, and thoughts allows us to be better in charge of our life. When we notice these subtle (and sometimes not-so-subtle) indicators we are better able to make small adjustments and get back into alignment before major breakdowns occur. And as we go further in this book, you'll hopefully see that we just keep circling back to our awareness. It is, after all, our greatest superpower!

Let's look at some possible indications of when grounding is needed:

- Easily overwhelmed by things that typically wouldn't shake you
- Feeling a sense of topsy-turvy, like you just can't get your bearings
- Lethargic and uninterested in activities that usually bring you joy; long bouts of apathy
- Experiencing a sense of chaos even when life is going well
- Easily triggered by trauma and trauma people
- Predominantly experiencing fear-based reactions
- Incessant need to control the outcome
- Believing that everything is dangerous
- Often experiencing paranoia without cause
- Having low energy in the body
- Digestion and elimination is slow, sluggish, or struggling
- Low sexual appetite
- Dizziness/vertigo
- Feeling clumsy or dropping things
- Issues with focus and streamlining your thoughts

Some indications of when centering is needed:

- Having the feeling that you are alone in the world
- Loss of faith, in any area, even in regards to yourself
- Having the sense of being abandoned in life, having abandonment issues in general
- Strong apathy or depression

- Headaches, migraines
- Dizziness/vertigo
- Being closed-minded to inspirations and creative ventures
- Uncharacteristic greed and materialism
- Having a sense of elitism
- Can play a role in many learning disabilities, comas, sleep disorders and mental illness.
- Being angry at [insert your deity here]

When you are anchored to the planet, filling your root chakra with Earth energy while simultaneously connecting to the energy that is Source, you are setting yourself up to be a perfectly balanced human being. The bridge between your physicality and spirit is indomitable. You are focused and alert as an individual, taking on the day-to-day challenges put before you in the microcosm. But you are also thriving in the knowing that everything is woven in the Divine Tapestry of the macrocosm. You have faith that tells you there's more to life than just being a human caught up in the daily grind. And that my dear, sets you up to have exactly the experience you came down to Earth to have in the first place. It's exquisite!

Inspired Assignment: Don't believe me? Try it for one week. Every day, ground and center, and pay attention to yourself as you navigate through life. Notice how you feel before, during, and after the exercise. Notice your stress levels, blood pressure, emotions, and mental disposition. Then, for the next few days forgo this exercise and compare the differences. Don't just take my word for it. Dare to try it on for yourself. Remember, just because it's easy doesn't mean it lacks value. This is the one step I never miss. Ever!

Final Thought

One last thing I'd like to mention. During this process, it's incredibly important to be gentle with yourself and have patience. You are rerouting energy, attention, and flow. It's like changing the direction a river travels. At first, it will probably feel like you're having to work really hard at it. You might find yourself feeling tired by the end of the day, even more so than usual. But this is perfectly normal because of the additional energy you are expending to remember and practice these techniques.

Piling on judgment and unrealistic expectations only adds pressure for you to perform and get it right. If at all possible, while playing with these new techniques, don't do that. Don't punish yourself for not getting it when you think you should be getting it. Marvel at the process. Be in the wonder of the magnificent creature that you are giving yourself the chance to be. Roll around in the joy that you are nourishing your body and soul. Celebrate that you are being proactive and setting yourself up to go beyond what you've ever had. That is what I ask you to focus on.

The trick is to not push too hard. There will be times when it's just not happening regardless of how open and expanded your imagination is. Take a break. Go for a walk. Clear your mind and come back and try again. You can't force this process. My Guys are great at always reminding me when I really want something but I'm forcing it to happen. They'll tap me on the shoulder and say "you're efforting again." That's my signal to let go of my attachment, relax a little bit, and just let it flow. Adding judgment and criticism will only add struggle and strife. Relax, play with it, and let it show you the way!

CHAPTER 3

Quiet

O ur world is busy. No doubt about it. It's filled to the brim with a constant stream of information, inundating us with a barrage of light, sound, and physical stimulation. We are pulled in every direction with demands and deadlines. It's a wonder we can focus on the tasks at hand or remain present in our conversations. The eyes and ears are soaking in everything they come into contact with. Sending tons of data to the brain for translation, filing, and storage.

Much of it we're not even aware of. It's more subconscious than we even know. So for all the things we are aware of, there are a billion other fragments of information we are not. And the brain is just drinking it all in. Then, when we finally do stop to take a breath and try to be quiet for a moment our minds race with thoughts, plans, and ideas. No wonder it's difficult to sleep after a really hectic day. The brain has much to share and we are finally stopping long enough to listen.

If the first breadcrumb focused on anchoring our energy with grounding and centering, the second breadcrumb on our journey - meditation - takes us to a place where we can be quiet and reflective. Where presence cultivates peace. A place where you are giving yourself the greatest gift. The gift of stillness.

Now before you go defending your excuses about how hard meditation is and why you can't sit still for that long, I want to throw out some new ideas to you about this ancient practice. Like I've stated before, I tend to not do what everyone else is doing. I find my own way. That includes adapting this sometimes-confusing practice into a practice that works. Over the years I've collected different concepts, techniques, and suggestions that have helped so many people find that space of stillness. As we navigate this chapter, let's explore these new possibilities together and see if meditation is as hard as you believe.

Hi, Me!

Throw away everything you think meditation is. Let's start from scratch. Toss it out! Right out of the window! Especially the idea that it's about shutting off your brain, quieting the ego, or leaving your "dirty human body" so that you can soar with the angels. Throw it all away. It's not accurate, and quite honestly, it's a little too "judge-y" for my taste. All of those ideas lend to the feeling that we are flawed and broken. That in order for us to reach a higher state of awareness, we must leave our human selves behind.

But really, that isn't fair. In their light aspect, our ego and humanness aren't wrong. They are doing a great job. They provide us the state of separatism so that we can experience this beautiful, physical adventure. The body is our vehicle to make delicious choices, feel pain, grow, hug, make love, float the river, eat, and to enjoy our time here. Hinting that we need to escape or shut it down tells the subconscious that we are not grateful for this human experience. It sends the message that something is wrong with us. So cut it out! Toss out your old ideas, and let's play with some new ones!

To me, meditation is the act of sitting with yourself, being quiet, and giving your attention to something specific. That's it. Simple. Pure. Easy. Okay, maybe not so easy, given the fact that we spend most of our days running around constantly distracted from that very thing. In general, we don't want to sit smack dab in the middle of who we really are. We invent ways to distract ourselves because, well, it can be difficult to see what's lurking in the shadows. To be so present with

44

who you are, to see your high points and low points, to come face to face with mistakes you've made and hearts you've broken...Yeah, it might not be so easy to just sit down and say "Sup?"

But part of what makes meditation so impactful is that it provides us the opportunity to accept who we are. Every bit of it. Icky parts and all. At first, you might find yourself being distracted or squirming a little because you're uncomfortable. That's okay. It's completely natural. That's just the ego resisting the meditation process because it's trying to protect you from the uncomfortable. In time and with some practice, you'll get the hang of it.

Side Note: Meditation doesn't require sitting still in the perfect lotus position, eyes closed, and hands in mudra position. You can do virtually anything from a meditative space. Some people do yoga or Pilates. Others prefer walking meditations. I noticed that I slipped into meditation while doing the dishes once. Really, it's just about focusing on yourself while being present to whatever you're doing. So, if sitting, eyes closed, legs crossed doesn't work for you, explore other ways to have quiet, reflective time with yourself. Whatever you choose to do, if you feel better afterwards, then you're doing it right.

Doing the Math

One of the internal conversational rabbit trails I frequent quite often sounds a little bit like this: My brain is essentially a biological computer, capable of collecting, storing, and translating data from all directions. I'm already making survivalist choices, sticking to my comfort zone, and knee-jerking my way through life based on the older programs that have been handed down to me through the years. As a child, I had no say in what programs were to be initially given to me. That was decided by my caregivers.

Now that I'm an adult, I have more power to choose the experiences I actually want. So, wouldn't it stand to reason that I could download my brain with new information? It's already working from programs I had no hand in creating. If I want to create a better habit with meditation, then why can't I program my brain to work towards that goal instead? Wouldn't it be possible to retrain it to do something productive rather than destructive? Wouldn't I be able to introduce a program called "Right now we're meditating?" Yes, as a matter of fact, I do believe I can. Since this biological computer is already designed to react and respond when certain stimuli are introduced, wouldn't it be safe to assume I could train it to respond with different, more consciously chosen stimuli?

The answer to all of these questions is YES! We are able to upgrade and redirect our brains to work in a way that supports us. We don't have to just accept what is. We are the masters of our experience! If you suddenly become aware of a habit or belief that doesn't support you, you are the very person to do something about it! This is the Divine Right of being born a human with free will. You are the one that is in charge of your experience. And this is precisely the moment you move from a reactionary, unconscious human to a proactive powerful being in this Universe! Game on!

The Ritual of Meditation

When I ask people if they meditate, the most common response I get back is how difficult it is getting the brain to be quiet. They tried meditation a few times but couldn't get past the clutter and noise, so they ended up feeling frustrated and flawed. Eventually, they gave up and moved on.

My take on it, though, is why are we trying to make our brain quiet? It's not made to be quiet. It is, in fact, designed to constantly think, offer logic and reason, and to answer questions. Its primary function is to fill in the gaps of a thought process that we don't have the answers to. It projects a viable path to take based on the data available, basically calculating the safest route to take when presented with various options. Yes, sometimes those thoughts run away like a wild stallion, but again, that can be trained. Forcing our beliefs on what it should or shouldn't be isn't very fair to the brain.

Instead, what if we took the approach of training the brain to take a break for us? Not forcing it to shut up but inviting it to just go out for coffee. If it's a programmable organ, let's program it to know when it's time to meditate. Let's give it the reassurance that it doesn't need it to be in charge in that moment and that we aren't in any danger. It gets the memo that this is just what we're doing, and there's no need to panic.

By giving the brain a ritual every day, something it can eventually count on, we redirect its natural pathway of providing constant facts and figures. Eventually, it learns to relax and naturally quiet down enough for you to explore the vastness within yourself. Haven't you noticed that when you try to push it down and force its silence, it only gets louder? So my suggestion would be, stop trying to exert your will on it and learn to work with it. As they say, you'll catch more flies with honey than you will with vinegar.

Before we go any further I want to take a moment to debunk the mystique of what a ritual is. Historically that word has gotten a bad rap, but it isn't as scary as you might think. According to Wikipedia: "A ritual is a sequence of activities involving gestures, words, and objects, performed in a sequestered place, and performed according to set sequence." (That's right! Wikipedia knows what's up!)

If you think about it, we conduct rituals every single day. From the order in which we get ready in the morning to our evening relaxation habits after our hectic day. Haven't you ever noticed you probably put on your shoes and socks in the same order each time? (I'm a left sock, left shoe, right sock, right shoe girl.)

Rituals for meditation can be created out of anything you want. It's your ritual. You're in charge. I suggest first creating a space in your home that is dedicated to meditation. Not your bed and not your favorite TV chair. Your brain is already programmed for specific activities in those areas. Choose a place that isn't used for anything else and set up a space that is relaxing and where you won't be disturbed. You may have a chair that you love, a few pillows on the floor, or maybe even a yoga mat or blanket. It doesn't matter so long as you feel comfortable and your body isn't being taxed. My favorite way to meditate is to take a pillow and put it under my bum, cross my legs and have two smaller pillows under my knees to lift them up slightly. This way I feel supported, my spine is straight and strong, and nothing hurts for the duration. If your body hurts, it will make it difficult to focus on anything else.

Another suggestion I have: Stack your body. Sit tall without slouching or leaning in any direction. Stack your head directly above your shoulders, your shoulders over your hips. Pop your butt out slightly and sit up tall as if a string was pulling your head up to the ceiling with your chin parallel to the floor. This allows not only for the natural curve of your spine but the life force energy that is in all of us will flow with greater ease. When our posture is lazy, our energy will be lazy.

Once I get into position and my pillows are all in place, I will then take a few deeps breaths to relax my body from the day and bring my awareness to myself. In that moment, I visually scan through my body to make sure I'm comfortable and nothing is stressed that might start hurting before I'm finished. I make any necessary adjustments, and then I'm good to go. I ground, center, take one last deep breath, and simply observe myself in that space.

This is my ritual. I do it every single time. It is my program for meditation, and thus, my brain is comfortable because it has learned nothing is wrong in this moment. It can relax because it now trusts the process and knows, "Oh we're about to meditate. I can take a break." You can have elaborate rituals such as lighting a candle or ringing a bell each time you sit down. You can start with a special prayer or an empowering chant. It doesn't matter what you do. Just do it each time. That's the programming part.

Let's say you try this but after a while you start feeling like the ritual you've chosen isn't quite resonating with you. Maybe you burn incense each time but you find that your sinuses don't like the smoke. Or perhaps the way you sit just isn't working for your body the more you practice. That's okay too. You aren't going to break anything if you choose a new ritual. Nothing is lost. You haven't done it wrong. I learned that if I burned my incense an hour before meditating, the smoke dissipated and I could breathe easier. And I can't tell you how many different positions I tried before I found just the right one for me. You don't have to throw out the whole ritual. Simply make small adjustments until you find your own style.

Side Note: Another common issue I hear from people is that they fall asleep when attempting to meditate. First, I do not recommend meditating while lying down, especially in the beginning. Your brain (and body) are programmed to sleep in that position already. So, there's a higher chance it will happen. Posture is important so find a way to sit tall, relaxed but alert. If you're sitting in a chair, move forward a bit so your back isn't resting on the chair back. Perch yourself on your sitz bones, the bony part of your booty. This keeps your mind alert so you don't fall asleep. You could also adapt your music if it's too soothing. Double check your fatigue level. Are you in need of a nap more than meditation? With a little troubleshooting and some minor adjustments, you'll find that perfect place of being completely relaxed but aware enough to stay awake.

Let's Take a Meeting

Back in the day, I used to do something that would set me up perfectly for meditation. I don't really know how this became my ritual, but it worked. I had a beautiful area I would sit in. I'd lay my pillows out, get all comfy, do my deep breathing, and ask my angels and guides to be present.

Once I was settled in, I'd let them have it! I'd let the words fly faster than a professional auctioneer. I would vent all the wrongs in my life, yelling to them, sometimes yelling *at* them. Anything and everything I was feeling I'd let fly out of my mouth. Whether it made sense or not, I just got it out.

The beautiful thing about our Guidance Team is that they don't get their feelings hurt nor do they take things personally. They're not tethered to an ego like we are so there is zero judgment about what we're saying or doing. Truly, they just want us to be honest about how we feel. Not because they don't already know but because they are providing the safe space for us to be honest with ourselves. And what a beautiful gift to offer a species that spends most of its time having hurt feelings, guarding what it says for fear of judgment, and holding back the truth because it's afraid of rejection. When a wounded human is truly seen and heard, healing occurs. Guides are very aware of this, which is why it is their honor to witness our journey and to be the space for whatever we need to heal.

Having successfully unloaded my word vomit, I would sit for a moment in the silence. I started to notice each time I did this exercise (actually, "exorcize" is probably more accurate), I would have more clarity about the situation and understand my part in it. After I dumped my hurt feelings about the situation I could see the nutrition it was providing. Once I reached that state, I would smile, say thank you to my guides, close my eyes, and go into my meditation. Because I had vented all of my thoughts and feelings in that moment, nothing was left to distract me. My brain was quiet. And the product afterwards was a closer relationship with my Guys. I knew they loved me enough to just let me be honest and they honored me by being present with where I was. A win-win all around!

Now What?

You've dedicated a space for your meditative exploration. You're comfortable and poised. You like the ritual you've chosen, and you feel you've got all the boxes checked off. But you still can't seem to get your brain to chill out! So now what?

It's going to take your brain a little time to understand that everything is okay. Our ego perceives anything that is uncomfortable as danger to its survival. When you decide to sit down, right in the middle of who you are, ready to witness the deepest part of your soul that might not be very comfortable. The ego will want to distract you because it thinks it will be dangerous. The brain inundates you with thoughts to get you to look away from the uncomfortable things. Now we've got to just calm it down and reassure it that it isn't in any danger. I know. It sounds silly, but let's give it a try.

Here's what worked for me. You know the digital ticker tape they use when updating stock prices? I see my thoughts on the ticker tape as they are running rampant. And it's my job to simply acknowledge the thought...that's right ACKNOWLEDGE it! Not shame it or shove it down. If you try to shut the brain down, it instantly turns into a two-year-old wanting mommy's attention. Prepare yourself for a world class tantrum! Complete with holding its breath and turning purple until you acknowledge what it wants. Trying to ignore something doesn't make it go away. Instead, we are going to have a calm, yet firm adult conversation with it.

This is literally the discussion I've had with my brain:

> Me: (a soft suggestion) Okay. Let's relax, breathe, and meditate.

> Brain: (ticker tape scrolls)
> thought/thought/thought/thought/thought

> Me: (a kind invitation) I hear you, but right now we're meditating. I'll get back with you when I'm done.

> Brain: (scrolling a bit slower)
> thought...thought...thought...thought...thought

> Me: (becoming insistent) Yup, got it. But right now, we're meditating. I'll get back with you when I'm done.

> Brain: (slower, but still persistent)
> thought......thought......thought......thought

> Me: (A bit more sternly) Right now we're meditating. I'll get back with you when I'm done.

> Brain: (almost there, it's surrendering)
> thought...........thought...........thought

> Me: (Firmly) Right now I'm meditating.

> Brain: thought......silence

When I acknowledge the brain but bring it back to the task at hand, as a loving mother might to her two-year-old, my thoughts begin to wane. My brain isn't in panic mode of needing my attention and starts to naturally relax. You may need to do this each time you meditate when just starting out. Eventually, you'll notice that when you sit and do your ritual in your favorite space, the brain will catch on and say, "Oh, that's right. We're meditating." No push. No pull. Just compliance.

Where You Go From Here

I've walked you through the "what" and "how," but the "what else" is up to you. If you prefer listening to music or sounds of nature, go for it. If you'd rather have a guided meditation playing for you to assist in a specific journey, do that. Or maybe silence is your chosen meditative canvas. Awesome! It doesn't matter. Try them all, find what works, and do that. How you get there, what you do, and where you go are all part of the excitement of a meditation journey. You can set a specific intention to receive guidance about a situation. You can ask to meet your spirit guides and/or angels. You could even go within and meet your inner child. Really, the options are limitless.

I generally will set an intention before I "go in." I'll open up to what my Guys have for me or will ask for some insight to a particular area of my life that has me stumped. The key here is to not go into meditation with a hard expectation of what you want. Anytime we attach to an expectation we set ourselves up for disappointment. Rather, try to have a relaxed frame of mind in this process. It's okay to have an idea of what you'd like to have happen, but try to remain open to receive what will best support you. You cannot force this process. And if you think I'm kidding, I'm not. Once I meditated and literally nothing happened. It was pure silence and pitch black. Later my guides told me *that* was what I needed. So that was what I received.

A great way to do this is by asking a particular archangel or spirit guide to assist you during your journey. My favorite one to call is Archangel Michael. He's bold, direct, and doesn't jerk you around but is always loving and supportive in your experience. I appreciate his candor. When I want it straight up, no holds barred, he's the one I call on. Or perhaps you feel more comfortable going straight to Source Energy (God/Goddess, YHWH, Jehovah, The All, etc.). Anything and everything is acceptable. You are only limited by your own limited thinking. So, be open and adventurous. Before long, you'll be traveling through dimensions on the wings of angels!

Loving Permission: Remember, too, some days will just be a struggle. Your day is already full of hectic schedules, helping your kids with their homework, your spouse can't finding this or that, shopping lists and deadlines will be floating around in your thoughts. Don't worry! Let it go. You can't force yourself to be in a peaceful space. It doesn't work like that. The more you push, the more frustrated you'll become. And that is exactly the opposite of what we are going for. So, just get up, take care of what needs taken care of, and come back later. Give yourself permission to not be in the right space for it and walk away. The last thing you want to do is berate yourself for not being perfect.

$\mathcal{A}$lign

Now that the foundation has been set and you've dedicated some time to connecting both your "human" and your "spirit" to their respective anchors, our next stop is the Chakra System! And honestly, it's one of my favorites. To me, it is the most important system for guidance that we have at our disposal. Its job is simple: to let us know how we're doing with the choices that we make. It is a real-time, internal navigation system, constantly reporting back to us along our journey. It does so by giving us physical and emotional indicators, moment-to-moment, as we maneuver through our free will existence.

The Whirling-Swirling World of Chakras

What is a chakra anyway? In layman's terms, it is an energy wheel within us that directs life force to a designated part of the body. The confusing part for people is that you cannot cut someone open and see them like you would an organ. And yet, even though they are invisible to the naked eye, they affect our physical bodies on a very real level.

The word chakra is derived from the Sanskrit word for "wheel" or "turning," but in the yogic context a better translation is "vortex" or "whirlpool." Imagine having thousands of tiny little whirlpools in your body, each one feeding an area of organs and tissues, nourishing that area with rich life force energy. When these "wheels" are in good working order, the body and emotions have a better sense of balance and focus in a continuously changing world. When one or more chakras are struggling, however, the energy flow will diminish and we will experience the effects in that section of our bodies as well as the correlating area of our lives.

There are thousands of them in our body and even a few within the space around us called the aura. But for the sake of this conversation, we'll be focusing on the seven main chakras while also adding the ear chakras just for good measure.

The Early Years...

When I began my spiritual journey oh-so-many years ago, I was enthralled with these invisible wheels of light. I read just about every book available, researched for hours on the Internet, and took chakra meditation classes any chance they were offered in my area. After a few months of this, I started to notice discrepancies that left me befuddled. Everyone had their own take on how big they are, how fast they spin, and in which direction. Some said they should all spin in a clockwise fashion. Others said counterclockwise, while some even stated they needed to alternate. Some books mentioned they needed to be the same size. Others claimed they all had their own unique size. It seemed I couldn't find a definitive answer and I got really, REALLY frustrated.

So, I threw it all away. I stopped reading what everyone else had written about the chakras, and I went within to ask them myself. I spent time in meditation, connecting with each one, feeling them out while working on seeing them with my inner vision. And yes, I would even talk to them. But that's not as crazy as the fact that they would answer me back. You heard me right. They actually talked back! It truly was a groundbreaking moment for me because that was the moment I began looking inward for my answers rather than taking everyone else's cues. This was a game changer!

I'm probably going to offend a lot of people with this comment, but personally, I really don't care which way they are spinning, the rate of their spin, or what color they are. Being an Empath, I'm much more interested in how they feel. Or, in turn, how I feel. If I'm aware of my feelings, sensations, and energy levels, I can better troubleshoot what is out of balance with them. And combining that with understanding the roles each chakra plays in my experience, I'm well on my way to being a proactive human and taking care of the issues as they arise. Therefore, I don't concern myself so much with what they look like. I'm more focused on how they are doing and what I can do to support them.

Making Friends with Myself

We humans are an interesting bunch. We are the only species that is emotionally abusive to ourselves while simultaneously being kind to others. We say the most horrendous things when no one is looking. It's such a common occurrence that I bet we hardly notice when we are doing it. And back in the day, I was really good at being really mean to myself. Since I grew up in a household that was negative and abusive, I grew into a young woman who had zero self-esteem, very little accountability, and hardly any awareness that I could be anything but that. Oh, I faked it pretty well, coming off as strong and even cocky at times. But it was all a hard candy shell covering the ooey-gooey center of my heart. And I hoped like crazy no one would figure that out.

I would typically fall into a ritual of self-abuse anytime I made a mistake in life, had a breakup, or felt I just wasn't good enough for XYZ. I would stand in front of a mirror, almost trance-like, usually crying, and say the most atrocious things to myself. As if I were scolding my inner child for breaking a favorite vase, the sharp, cutting words would pour out of me. Looking back, I can see how it would satisfy something in me, like it would give me some sort of "fix," breaking my spirit until the numbness would set in. Once I was all "filled up," I would spend the rest of the day numb.

But one fateful day I saw myself, standing in front of the mirror, speaking the words. Like, *really* saw myself for the first time. I couldn't believe I was actually saying these things. Out loud! And the pain in my heart was so deep, I was surprised I wasn't aware of it before. Something had finally clicked and I had no more interest in harming myself in such a manner. That was the last time I participated in that ritual. I still remember the moment like it was yesterday, burned into my brain as a reminder to be gentle with myself.

Fast forward a bit. Around the time I began working with my chakras, I thought about that old habit and how easy it was to be so mean to myself. Yet, I knew in my heart, I would have never said those things to another person. Which got me to thinking...if I treated my chakras as if they were individual people, then I would be more apt to listen to them, support them, and love them. Which, by proxy, I would then love myself, since my chakras really are just me anyway. By visualizing them as individual people, say my best friends, I would be loving myself. Bingo!

In my mind, I quite literally see them as eight different people, all different ethnicities and genders. (I have eight because I added the ear chakras, remember?) They all wear color coordinated shirts, reflecting the traditional chakra colors and each have their own unique personalities. I know that sounds weird, but I don't care. It works for me, and that's the point right? It never matters how you get where you're going as long as you feel good when you get there. And it's especially important to have fun doing it.

Conversations with Chakras

Here's what I've learned during my chats with these swirling wheels of light. Our chakras are designed to support us in our Earthly adventures. Each one monitors specific areas of our life and aids us in our decision-making process. They each have their own specialty and yet work well with each other to create a complete navigational system. They are a part of our overall committee that is in place at the moment of our birth. (The committee I'm talking about at this point is comprised of our Chakra and Four Body Systems, our Higher Self, ego and our innate intuition. All of which we'll be discussing further as we continue.)

The Chakra System works like a fire alarm that alerts us when we've made a choice that doesn't truly support our Highest Good. The alarm is soft at first, hoping to gently get our attention by saying, "Hey, did you really mean to do/say that?" It might come to us as a slight pressure in the body. Maybe it manifests as an emotion washing over us. It could even be a nagging gut instinct that bugs us for a couple of days. Regardless of how the alarm sounds, it is up to us to pay close enough attention to acknowledge it and correct our behavior as best as we can. But more often than not, we are too busy, too stressed, and/or too distracted to notice the alarm. We end up moving on with our day, pushing the feeling down and trying to cope.

Living in a modern medical society we have been trained to seek medication for our discomfort rather than investigate the whole body for the root cause. In this country especially, it's more acceptable to get a prescription than to sit quietly and ask our body what is going on. We typically squash things that show up as discomfort by taking a pain pill or an antacid if our body isn't working like we want it to. We might think we're stressed and overworked and in need a good night's sleep to feel better. Or we go as far as numbing ourselves with alcohol, drugs, or even using television or sex as a distraction to quiet that nagging feeling. More often than not, we are all just trying to get through life without really asking the questions that will bring us the truth. Sometimes, it's just easier to ignore them. Or so we think.

Again, we are standing face-to-face with the conversation of self-awareness, yet going into another level of how important this practice can be and how it might support our overall health and well-being. There isn't anything else that will ever support you more than being present while you are living your life. And that's exactly why I love working with the Chakra System. It truly is our navigational beacon along the journey of life. Due to the fact that we are free will beings fueled by stories, misperceptions, and ego-based desires, we can make a lot of stupid decisions. But the Chakra System is there to help guide us through the multitude of choices we face on a daily basis.

> "I may not have gone where I intended to go, but I think I have ended up where I needed to be."
> - Douglas Adams, The Long Dark Tea-Time of the Soul

Road Trip!

Because the Chakra System is in place to be our navigation, I see it very much like the dashboard in a vehicle. That dashboard is designed to give the driver early warnings when something isn't working properly. If you're on a long road trip and your oil light comes on you don't just ignore it, do you? No, you pull over and give your car a big ol' swig of oily juice. Then it comes back into balance and the light turns off. That little red light is the first step to let you know your vehicle needs servicing. Ignore it and over time, the vehicle will begin to get your attention with clunking noises and eventually engine problems. Ignore it further and the motor will seize up, lock and crack, and then you're screwed.

Quick Story: I've actually done that. Remember the part where "my mom didn't give me very good tools for life?" Well, I was never told I had to put oil in my car. So, I ended up driving my first car to its limits, bone dry and all. Eventually, clunk clunk clunk, dead. Looking back, it's so silly for me to NOT know the engine needs these things. But we don't know what we don't know, until we do. Then we know. That's why I'm glad you're here. So we can have these open discussions and know these tools together.

That's exactly what the chakras do for us. They let us know how we're doing on the road trip of life. They monitor our choices, words, feelings, and thoughts. When we do or say things that serve our Highest Good, we have alignment and all is well. Step out of that alignment and our Chakra System will give us a little red light, warning us that we've made a choice that doesn't work. Our job is to get good at paying attention to catch that warning. The sooner you catch it, the sooner you can clean it up, putting yourself back into alignment. And really, by alignment I mean being in sync with your own internal integrity. But to better illustrate what I mean, I want to take you through the chakras, one-by-one to explain it a bit further.

Cleaning It Up: I want to expand a little bit about what this statement means. It takes a brave soul to look at their mistakes, missteps, and messy mishaps. More often than not, people ignore and deny they've had a hand in anything that goes awry. But truly, alignment thrives when we take responsibility and have accountability for the part we play in our relations. Even when that means it didn't go as well as we would have liked.

Cleaning it up means just that. First, taking ownership of your part. And only your part. Not taking it all and not pointing the finger at anyone else. Simply looking at yourself, your choices, and your actions. When you realize you made a mess, clean it up. Go apologize. Offer support to those you hurt by helping clean up your mess. Make amends with your own integrity. And lastly, forgive yourself for the misstep. Once you've done all you can do, let it go and promise yourself you'll work to do better. By taking this bold step to not curtail your mistakes, you are taking a strong stance in being an aligned, integral human.

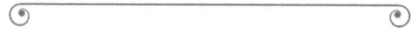

Let's Break it Down

I'm not going to spend too much time on ALL the attributes, coordinating systems and organs, and physical ailments of chakra imbalance. All the books I talked about before, yeah, that information is there. Go nuts! I much more prefer spending time talking about the relationship you can have with them. I'd rather focus on how you and your chakras work together to support your overall alignment as a whole. That's where the conversation gets juicy! So let's break it down, from root to crown. Hey, that rhymes!

ROOT
Location: Pelvic Floor, Tailbone Area

Not to play favorites, but for me the root chakra is the most important one in the whole system. Its main focus is to stabilize and nurture our feelings of safety and security, monitoring the calculations of survival and/or danger of demise. As a human, our root is crucial because we generally run a high level of fight-or-flight response to our surroundings as it is. And if we don't feel safe and secure, we typically don't thrive in life. Additionally, if fear is the dominant emotion running, the other chakras will respond in kind. Just like a string of lights, when the root shuts down the others will follow suit and shut down as well. All to conserve their energy and stay safe. So that's where we start.

When one's root is balanced, connected, and stable life just seems to work. Even when it's coming at you from all directions. A balanced root provides a sense of calmness within the storm, almost having you feel like you can look out at the world and say "I've got this" in your best superhero voice. The root anchors your energies into the planet, giving you nourishment from Mother Earth. This feeds the body and calms the fears that bubble up inside.

Food for Thought: There are two ways a chakra can be out of balance. The first is when we experience long periods of fear-based living. Whichever area of life we are afraid of, the correlating chakra will shrink in size and become sluggish. If we believe the stories of our fears we tend to be less proactive, causing the chakra to feel unsupported. It now has to fend for itself and will make itself smaller for protection.

Another way it becomes imbalanced is when we are obsessed about a particular area of life and we give it too much aggressive focus. The relating chakra will then become engorged and inflamed. The system gets choked out and our navigation through life is clouded with anger and aggression.

Example: Tommy grew up in a verbally abusive household and could never speak up in his own defense. As a child his throat chakra closed down from fear and left him with very little to say when he was upset. As he grew up, he harbored resentment and anger towards his abusive parents as well as others like them. Until one day, all of that anger boiled up and exploded in a tyrannical rant of destruction. It felt good to be able to finally express himself. But in an attempt to find his voice he swung the pendulum so hard to the other side that now the chakra has too much energy. Tommy may be able to express himself but now it comes out as anger.

When one chakra becomes inflamed, it will choke out its neighbors. In Tommy's case, his throat chakra is so engorged it spills over into the heart chakra space, choking out compassion and forgiveness. It also covers his third eye chakra, clouding his perception about the situation at hand. This feeds him with justification that aggression is needed and he doesn't care if he hurts someone in the process. All that matters is that he will never be silenced again!

The energy will cease to flow in that area of the body when we don't allow energy to flow in that area of our life. See how they work? Your chakras directly respond to your moment-by-moment choices and the correlating areas of your external experience. And where it's extremely common for humans to "pendulum swing" like this, living in either extreme for too long is out of balance.

When a person experiences large chunks of their day afraid of life, fearing risk, and disconnected from the knowing that they are safe in general, their root will shrink. It will collapse upon itself in order to conserve its energy for survival. When it comes to our mortality a small target is hard to hit. And once that process begins the rest of the system will follow suit. One by one, the chakras shrink down, closing in and causing restriction in the natural flow.

When people are obsessed with survival the root will become engorged and angry, giving the person strong feelings that death can come at any minute and they had better be prepared. A good example of how that looks are the people that call themselves "doomsday preppers." Their fear of dying has grown into a determination to survive. There is almost an aggressive obsession with survival, having them pump the root with fear and anger energy, causing it to swell, and choking out the neighboring sacral chakra.

SACRAL
Location: Two inches below navel

The sacral chakra oversees your passion in life. All kinds of passion: art, food, wine, chocolate, sex, jumping out of airplanes, etc. It is your creative center and we are passionate creation beings...we must make stuff! This is the space where we want to explore life's possibilities and make our mark in the world. With the root having us feel all cozy and safe, the sacral will have us taking chances by creating something beautiful in the world. Perhaps the mark you want to make is in creating art. You'll feel safe enough to put yourself out there for the world to see. Or if that passion burning in your soul is to be a musician, nothing is going to get in your way of making music for all to hear.

When the sacral is out of whack there are "passion issues." I personally believe this is where addiction is born. It's just my theory but here's how it looks. In the root, its goal is to have you feel safe and supported. Then there's the sacral wanting to experience life at its fullest by expressing itself with passion and creativity. When these two are small and weak, humans will experience a larger amount of fear, and in response, will live a very small life. They will think they just don't matter and will be consumed by feelings of having low worth and being insignificant, leaving them to live a life of low risk.

But since humans crave the need to feel safe and comforted, the sacral will kick in its self-soothing instincts around the passion/pleasure center. It starts to overcompensate, overlapping the neighboring root and solar plexus chakras. People will grab onto something external to give them comfort, since the root isn't providing a sufficient amount. The sacral literally tries to be the surrogate soother to the root, trying to calm it down by grasping onto anything that will create the illusion of stability.

Depending on other factors in the individual's life history, they'll choose their "drug of choice." Drugs or alcohol, even sex or shopping, whatever it is that will soothe them at that time. For me, that sometimes looked like abusing myself verbally in a mirror until I was numb to the self-loathing. But whatever it is, it's important to understand that it is a false sense of safety. You know when they say, "That will never fill the void?" That's what they mean. Addiction never truly feeds the person. It only temporarily soothes the internal fear and instability they are experiencing at the moment.

Working with the grounding exercises for the root will begin to stabilize the fear one feels. Then, that peace will start to flow into the sacral and hopefully, mellow out its obsession for safety in things that don't provide safety at all.

SOLAR PLEXUS
Location: Just below rib cage near diaphragm

The solar plexus (SP) rules over our willpower, sets healthy boundaries, births conviction, and is the space from which our beliefs get carried out into the world. It is the powerful human in action! And where these qualities may appear a bit disjointed in relation to each other, they actually flow quite nicely as a team. To be a human in action for others we must first have conviction of self. In that conviction we carry the belief that our acts of service have value. That stance will naturally formulate into healthy boundaries because we aren't going to let others deter us from the mission we so passionately believe in. We will stand proudly on whatever soapbox we choose, believing in our message and capable of deflecting the ridicule from others so to not lose our balance. Powerful human, indeed!

When the SP is withered, a person might have lax boundaries, playing the role of doormat and letting anybody and their dog walk all over them. Conviction in who they are will be in question, constantly doubting their abilities and self-worth. Their belief in themselves will fade and they will simply exist. Over time, lethargy and apathy will set in as they question their ability to be an active participant of their own existence.

When the SP is enlarged, well now, we have a whole other bag of issues. Big-wig CEOs and politicians are great examples (generally speaking, of course). People that are so power hungry that they will do anything to get to the top – including hurting others in the process. Their SP is overlapping their creative and passion center (sacral), giving them the exaggerated sense that success is their passion when really it's their addiction. Simultaneously, it chokes out compassion for others (heart), which disconnects them from feeling empathy for anyone they step on as they climb the ladder of success. It numbs out their heart-to-heart connection, and they are blinded by their passion to succeed.

Quick Glance: These first three chakras are considered the physical/human chakras. They support and monitor the physical experience of being human. When we are grounded, we feel safe and secure, and that flows into the sacral where we love life and want to put our creations into the world. The sacral then spills into the SP where our conviction and belief are powerful motivators for us to be in action while we cultivate healthy boundaries. Balancing these three chakras has us feeling happy, healthy, and in alignment. We are clear, passionate, and focused as we step boldly in the direction of being the spirited human we were born to be.

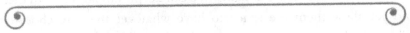

HEART

Location: Center of chest, near physical heart

Ever heard the saying "the heart of the matter?" It means to center of the issue. That's because our heart chakra *is* our center. It's our connection beyond the physicality, beyond what is logical and mundane. It is our connection beyond what we can see and hear. It is our internal wisdom. The heart chakra houses our emotions. ALL of the emotions. Meaning they are all valid, not the just "fluffy-bunny" ones. Emotions are indicators of how we're doing in our experience. But we tend to only want to focus on the happy, positive ones, denying and almost vilifying the ones we judge negatively. I get it. We like being happy. Advertisers spend billions of dollars every year to project messages that we'll be happy if we just buy their stuff.

But just because you feel sad or angry in that moment doesn't mean it's wrong. It means you are getting a signal to take a look at what's going on and troubleshoot your choices. Your heart is *your* center. If it doesn't feel good, take a moment to ask what's happening. *Really* ask. Rather than, "Why is this happening to me?" in a "wah-wah" victim-type voice, ask it in an inquisitive English Professor kind of voice instead. Sometimes, just changing the tone shifts everything. You'll be surprised. You might get an answer.

And while I'm at it, asking better questions helps a lot, too. Ask things like, "I wonder what message is trying to get my attention," and "What am I getting out of this experience?" Shifting your intention, tone, and receptivity will help greatly in understanding why you're having that bumpy experience.

When the heart chakra is open and flowing, we love. Simple. We are connected with other humans. We can deeply empathize with them and yet allow them the space to have whatever they are choosing. When the heart is shrunken, we can be guarded and cold-hearted. Sometimes people will be hard and jaded about life. Others might take on the role of victim or martyr. It will really depend on the individual and what life experiences they've had that hurt their heart in the first place. As with all of these examples, they are just general possibilities. We are not cookies. We aren't all cut out the same.

Another indicator when the heart is small is overcompensating by giving too much love. These people tend to be the fixers, rescuers, and enablers. They are the ones that will do anything for anyone just to be loved in return. Of course, they don't realize this is their motive. They think they are helping by giving all they have. But it isn't helping anyone. Instead it is co-dependency and manipulation. Harsh words, I know. But let's call it what it is. If Sally didn't get love from her mother, and of course, it breaks her heart, she will try the rest of her life to prove she is lovable. She'll live out her days loving people so much, so hard that it actually runs them off. (Because let's face it, people can feel the desperation.) Alternatively, some will stick around and take advantage of the energy she's giving. But it isn't really love; they're just using her. Unaware and driven by her obsession, she gives even more, until she's empty. And the motive? Sally is giving it all to others so that they hopefully give back to her to prove her mother was wrong…manipulation. And that never works. Ever! By the way…I'm Sally. Yup. Been there, lived that, got the T-shirt. And after a few thousand tries I burned the damn thing!

The engorged heart chakra might show itself through anger and rage. I personally believe anger is a valuable, sacred emotion. It marks the moment when we decide to make a powerful change, and we just simply won't stand for the same old, same old. But when someone just spews their anger without actually healing the wound from which it comes, their anger is explosive. I see these people: They're like the quintessential old man screaming at the kids to get off his lawn.

An engorged heart chakra never works properly physically or emotionally. The pent up anger can manifest itself in explosive defensiveness and lack of compassion. Over time, the physical heart will struggle due to the unresolved anger, showing up as signs of cardiopulmonary issues.

The neighboring chakras suffer, too. As the heart overlaps the SP, what was once healthy boundaries will turn to hardened walls. The angry old man is ready for a fight as his body becomes rigid. His perception of others becomes skewed as he overreacts to misunderstandings and closes off to the possibility of clearing up the disagreement.

A swollen heart also influences the throat chakra by expressing itself in anger and frustration for those misunderstandings rather than from a place of empathy. This state disconnects the person from their own authentic voice and puts them in an aggressive and dominating communication style.

THROAT
Location: Neck and Shoulder Region

Your throat chakra is your communication center. It governs your verbal expression, your actual voice. It is also responsible for how you express yourself through your body language as well as your inner self-talk. It's all communications. I was even surprised at how true that is while writing this book. My throat chakra would feel "tired" if I had been writing several days in a row, even though I would go hours without speaking.

There are two main styles of verbal communication, the authentic voice and what I call, brain speak. Both are valid and each has its place depending on the situation. But humans tend to speak from the brain more often without even being aware of it. Our calculating communication habits galvanize as we begin to trust our logic and reason over our internal wisdom. This leaves us disconnected from our lower chakras and relying on ego-based methodology to stay safe.

But the balanced human will feel safe and secure (root), will be passionate and creative (sacral), definitely will want to be in action with all that yumminess swirling about (solar plexus), love who they are and will easily connect with others (heart). This balance will naturally come out of their throat as the authentic voice. No thinking required. No logic and reason, no calculations to figure out. It will just spill out perfectly. The perfect expression of self at any given moment.

Brain speak is when we are calculating our words, trying to say just the right thing that will have us be accepted rather than rejected. It's methodical and safe. It isn't that it's wrong to communicate this way. It's usually a survival technique and not a thriving type of expression. We've adapted over the years to not let our hearts be exposed and vulnerable. We did that a few times and it got crunched and chomped, right? That trauma set us up for speaking from the brain. Communicating from the brain is where we can calculate and stay safe. Brain speak doesn't hurt as much, and yet we aren't saying what we really want to say. It's an incomplete way to communicate; it's not authentic. It's manufactured.

And know too, there are times when it's best to choose your words carefully and speak from the brain. You might have a boss who's abrasive and tyrannical at times but telling him to take a flying leap isn't necessarily a great career choice. Or perhaps you are in a PTA meeting and one mother won't shut up about her perfect daughter. Sometimes, it's best to smile, nod, and let the leader direct the flow of conversation.

With all that said, there is always a way to communicate the truth without harm. We have the ability to say what we really feel while holding the intention of not hurting anyone in the process. We've just lost our trust in our abilities to do so. The mastery is in finding your authentic voice even in times when you don't think you can. You say exactly what is on your mind (or heart) and deliver it in such a way that the other person receives it. Even if it's something that's difficult to hear. Squelching your voice is never going to work for you in the end. It just might take you a little time to find the right words.

When the throat is shrunken our voice will be small. We'll have a tendency to not share our opinions, passions, and concerns. We'll struggle to say no when our boundaries are stepped on, allowing people to walk all over us. On the other end of the spectrum, our ability to say yes won't be in very good shape, either. There is a tendency to sabotage the good things in life just as much as we allow bad things from our lack of boundaries. Bottom line, when we are disconnected from our true voice, our ability to communicate what is best for us gets messed up, tangled, and confused.

When a throat is enlarged and inflamed, our voice will be too strong and aggressive. Go back to our example with Tommy and how he finally found his voice but now it's too harsh. These people have finally found their "no," but they haven't healed the reason that their "no" was lost to begin with. The pendulum swings too far, from meek to abusive. Inevitably, their throat chakra overlaps their heart, cutting off compassionate connection with others. It also covers the third eye, skewing their perception and justifying their aggression. It's a vicious cycle.

THIRD EYE
Location: Center of Forehead

The third eye houses what you see, what you think you see, and how you feel about seeing it. Simply put, it is your perception of what you experience. Oddly enough, what you observe isn't always what really happened. Perception is a tricky bitch that way. Our brain starts making up stories about what we just witnessed in order to better categorize it. It will create conclusive thoughts (judgments), will calculate if fight-or-flight is needed (communicating with the root), and will have you respond based on similar past experiences (archived emotions in the heart). But what if none of that really happened? Big question, huh? *mind blown* This would definitely be one of those moments where my Guys would step in a say, "Just the facts, ma'am."

The third eye works like the film library of a movie production company. It records everything your eyes witness and how you felt when seeing it, storing the information away for future reference. Example: Roberta witnessed a fatal shooting as a young child. The deceased was someone she knew and cared about greatly. Her heart feels the emotion as she witnesses the attack and will get stored in her subconscious library alongside the film.

Fast forward a few years, she is watching a movie and a gun fight breaks out. This might trigger something in Roberta, reminding her (sometimes subconsciously) of her own traumatic experience when she lost her loved one. The third eye sees what is currently happening and will pull from the library of what it remembers as a reference point. The brain kicks on, telling stories about the present experience by comparing it to the past one. As Roberta remembers, the heart gets triggered by the traumatic emotions of the past event. This causes her to feel the same in the present moment as she did back then. At this point logic has no say. The brain is trying to explain how the movie has nothing to do with Roberta's past trauma. But the trigger will override logic and cause her to react to the movie, nonetheless. She'll more than likely experience emotional swings, physical and chemical reactions, and possibly a panic attack. In essence, she will be living the past in the present moment. This is what we now call Post Traumatic Stress Disorder (PTSD).

When the third eye is balanced and the root is grounded, our reaction to trauma and trauma triggers is minimized. It sees beyond the perception and can work through the trigger without painful reactions. The human isn't locking themselves into just one point of view of what is happening. They see the expansiveness of their experience, witnessing many layers within that one moment in time.

73

And even if they do experience emotions from that trigger, they will still likely have enough self-awareness to be able to allow the emotions to flow and not be overcome by them.

A closed third eye is the opposite. The human will be extremely limited in their viewpoints, rigid, in fact. "Hard headed" people have smaller third eyes. They aren't open to seeing new possibilities or experiencing alternative viewpoints from other people. The enlarged third eye might look a lot like the closed one, but they will be more aggressive about their perception. The smaller chakra comes across as "victim-y." And the larger one will encroach upon the throat, crown, and ear chakras making it just a big ol' mess all around! That cuts out being open-minded (crown) and hearing other people's viewpoints (ears), as well as being aggressive and argumentative (throat). Not my favorite person to hang out with.

EARS

Location: Just above physical ears

Not everyone includes the ear chakras in their books, but I really like giving them their moment in the sun as well. After all, clairaudience is one of my favorite superpowers so they deserve time to shine with the other chakras. The ear chakras are located directly above your physical ears on either side of your head. Picture Shrek. Yeah, they're like that.

Working in the same manner as the third eye, the ear chakras collect and file away the experiences you hear along with the correlating emotional responses deep within its auditory library. These experiences are stored within the subconscious and anytime you are triggered by sound this is the library those memories are pulled from.

Go back to the example of our dear Roberta. This time she is walking down the street when suddenly she hears a car backfire. The stored perceptions of what that sound means will have her react in a fearful way because of the past experience of trauma. The brain recognizes the sound, pulls from the auditory library as a reference point, and triggers physical/emotional responses. Again, logic has no power of reason when it comes to trauma triggers. She is well aware that it was a car and not a gun that made the noise. But her subconscious trauma has won over her logical mind and she reacts.

The third eye and ear chakras work together to house the full memory of our experiences. One being visual and the other auditory, both collecting emotions, stories, and interpretations. We can be triggered by both or either, depending on the person and situation. The tricky part though, is we aren't always fully aware that we are reacting to something buried deep within. Sometimes we react to external stimuli but don't always know the trauma in our library the subconscious is referring to. Practicing self-awareness helps to catch when our over-reactive responses don't match what is currently in front of us.

Open and healthy ear chakras will look a lot like a person with a healthy third eye. That person is open to hearing other perspectives, opinions, and viewpoints. They aren't rigid around their own beliefs and will honor others in their self-expression. And yet at the same time, they are capable of communicating their own viewpoints and opinions with respect.

In turn, whether the ears are shrunken or engorged, the result looks much like the person with third eye issues. They really do go hand in hand in my experience, only one is the visual receiver and the other is auditory.

CROWN
Location: Top of the head

The crown chakra is the polar opposite of the root. It houses your spiritual connection where the root is your human/physical connection. The crown oversees your tether to the Divine, whatever you choose to call that: God, Goddess, the Universe, Spirit, or even Spaghetti Monster. It is your direct line to Source. And to be perfectly frank, you don't even have to believe in a "Supreme Being" to have a healthy crown. The state of the chakra isn't dependent on whether or not you subscribed to a belief system. One can have faith without praying to a deity. It's how much you believe in whatever you believe in. Which means it also communicates with your solar plexus and fortifies those beliefs with personal conviction and action. This is what motivates people to stand for what they believe in.

People with "God issues," who have been abused by clergy, or who harbor anger and resentment for their religious experiences can have smaller crown chakras. The unresolved issues settle into the crown, causing the chakra to shrink and disallow connection from a spiritual source. In some way, it seems the human shuts this area down in order to protect themselves from future religious harm.

Keep in mind these are general statements and won't apply to all people. In fact, some agnostics and atheists can actually be quite balanced in the crown. It's not the belief system or lack thereof that causes the disturbance. The crown becomes imbalanced when the person carries wounds from religious or spiritual trauma and they have not properly addressed them. The emotions will fester in the "basement of your house," and the crown will simply do its best to get your attention so that you can heal those wounds.

Those with an inflamed crown are the people that believe they *are* God. Extremist cult leaders and self-righteous clergy will have an enlarged crown that clouds their perception of not only who they are

76

but who/what God is in relation to them. It gets muddy in the mind and they will start to personify their chosen deity. To further exacerbate this, the ego is also housed in the brain so it further supports their faith in themselves being the "Second Coming."

When the crown flourishes, there is a feeling that something bigger is in play. There is a contentment, a knowing that whatever we may be going through at the time, somehow will work itself out. This too shall pass as they say. The root provides the microcosm awareness, our immediate moment in time. The crown supports us in the bigger picture. It's the macrocosm. When these two chakras work in unison, there is harmony between our human and spiritual halves. We are present to the best choices that will serve our physical experience, but we have faith that it will all be okay. There is peace that comes from within. We are safe and secure and life is good.

Quick Glance: In review, we have the lower three chakras (root, sacral, and solar plexus) supporting and nourishing our physical/human connection. The upper chakras (throat, third eye, ears, and crown) are considered the spiritual chakras. They connect us to information that inspires and guides our life. The heart connects them in the center. Looking at the whole picture, it is our emotions that bridge the physical and spiritual realms. When we are inspired by Spirit we are uplifted by the emotional response and will put those inspirations into action. And when the human experiences the emotional response to a choice, we can better navigate towards what supports our Highest Good. It is the perfect dance of a divinely-inspired human life!

Systems Unite!

There they are, in all their individual and relating splendor. The chakras compute and translate our experiences in their respective specialties, witness how we're doing and what we're choosing, and then let us know if it works or not. Ever-so diligently monitoring the days and nights, the ups and downs, the highs and lows. Lovingly supporting us to choose the path that flows. Hey, that rhymes too!

Our job is to simply pay attention, check in often, and do our best to troubleshoot when they need our help. After all, we are on the same team. By implementing a systems-check practice we stand a better chance at remaining aligned, aware, and alert in life.

To better illustrate this, let me give you a step-be-step glimpse into my own process:

- During random check-in's throughout the day, I recognize, "something is up." When a chakra is in distress, it will give me a signal. It feels light at first, like a slight grab or ache. If I catch it, I go to the next step. If I don't, the chakra will continue to increase its intensity until I do. That's the beauty of their determination to assist us with our alignment. They don't give up on us. We are a team.

- Once I feel something might be out of whack, I stop and acknowledge it. Literally, I ask the chakra if everything's okay. I might even pat that chakra in a comforting way to connect further. Remember, I see them as my best friends. How would you comfort your best friend if they were in distress?

- Then, I think about what that chakra rules over. Typically, my throat is the first one to get my attention when I've either said something I didn't want to say or didn't say something I needed to. It will get that weird "froggy" thing within minutes. When it does, I stop and review the past few minutes.

- Now to investigate. I call this backtracking. Going backwards in time, I'll look where I might have said something/didn't say something that was out of alignment for me. I review until I find it. Sometimes, it's easy. Sometimes, I have to do a little digging, depending on how long the throat has been trying to get my attention. I may not always catch it, and at times, I struggle with figuring it out. Don't stress. Just do your best. But above all, be honest. This is the portion of the game called "owning your part." It's not always pretty, but you'll respect yourself more if you do.

- If I don't figure out what I did/didn't do, I will talk with my chakra, committing to do better next time and will do whatever I need to have it feel supported and healed. I might drink some yummy tea while pondering my commitment to being more present with my words moving forward. Or I might spend some time creating conscious mantras that support my authentic voice. Anything that is loving and supportive. This isn't the time to scold yourself for not being perfect. That will only cause the throat to have more stress. Remember, internal communication is still communication.

- If I do figure it out, I then go into my heart and ask it directly what I need to do to clean it up. It sounds strange and you will probably feel weird the first few times. But if you can stay open to hearing the heart, you just may. This is the game called "cleaning up your shit." You do whatever you need to do to put that chakra back into alignment. That's your job. The chakra's job is to tell you that it's out of alignment. Yours is to put it back. Whatever that is. You might need to have a conversation with someone letting them know they hurt you, giving you an excellent opportunity to speak your truth and reinstate your boundaries. Or you could be the one that owes them an apology, giving you the chance to strengthen your relationship and reinstate trust with them. It doesn't matter what it is. Just figure it out and do it. That will give your chakra the message that you're on its side and that it is loved, nurtured, and supported. (YOU will be doing this for YOU!)

- Once I've done all I can do, I do my best to forgive myself for my part in it. On some level, I know I have participated in whatever happened. If the other person is the one that transgressed and we both feel satisfied with our conversation about it, I forgive them. I might need to strengthen my boundaries or I may just simply need to release the energy of it. If I'm the one that messed up I work towards forgiving myself. Basically, you are taking charge and giving your entire being whatever it needs to get back into alignment with who you know yourself to be. The end goal is to walk away from that situation feeling clean. You know that you have done what needed to be done for your Highest Good. It's not always easy work, but I promise it is definitely worth it!

The chakras are an amazing gift to humanity. These beautiful balls of energy are constantly watching out for us. And even though they are quite capable of self-regulating they can't do everything all the time. Yes, they are hard-wired to work for you. And they do. Very well, in fact. They perform round the clock, diligently without fail. Each masterfully playing their role to enhance your beautiful human experience upon this Earth. But, they aren't responsible for the whole dang thing. They need your proactive support. They need to know you're on their side just as much as they are on yours. Getting involved in your own life and being a proactive participant is how you support them. Making decisions that work for you is how they thrive. Listening and acknowledging when you've gotten off track is powerful. Honoring them for the guidance they provide and choosing what serves your Highest Good...THAT is a healthy relationship with the whole being that you are.

CHAPTER 5

Radiate

Hopefully, at this point you are able to see the structure of your totality coming into view. The grounding and centering cords are anchored, secured, and providing you with some leverage in this crazy world. You've been giving yourself some quiet time to be present to your internal wisdom through meditation (in whatever form that resonates). Rounding you out nicely is the Divine Energy that's pumping through your Chakra System and flooding your body with radiant nutrition. All of these components, working in unison, with clockwork-like precision comprises your internal structure. It is everything that keeps you connected, aware, and working in tip-top shape. Combined with your diligence for checking in, expanding your awareness, and making choices that work for you, you are becoming quite the specimen. With all the cogs fitting nicely together, you are a well-oiled machine, working perfectly to guide and direct the spirited human in the direction that serves the Highest Good. Well done, you!

The next and final system we'll be covering in the beautiful existence that is YOU is the Four Body System. Much like the Chakra System, this uniquely layered bubble of energy plays a role in your day-to-day navigation.

The Perfect Bod

Ah, the aura. That beautiful innate field of energy that surrounds the physical body. We all have one, nobody is exempt. It comes with the package deal of being born on this planet. Those familiar with this bubble of energy like to focus their attention on the aura's colors and to appoint meaning to the varying hues. Yes, it is true, with special equipment we can see the many colors that comprises our auric field. For me though, much like the chakra colors, I don't really care what color the aura is. It is ever-shifting and changing based on our current disposition, anyway, so the colors aren't as important as our responsibility in maintaining our alignment. (Chakra and aura color people, please don't hate me. I still love you!) The colors simply reflect what is happening in our mind, body, spirit, and heart at that moment in time. If we were to meditate, exercise, have sex, or think about the pile of emails waiting for us on Monday, it would shift the colors immediately. So again, I tend to focus on how I feel versus how they look, since how they look is simply a snapshot in time.

There are many layers to the aura reaching far past our immediate space. I prefer focusing on the first four, however, as I feel this is the area where we can directly affect by making free will choices. Each one of these layers acts as a filter, relaying information through our Chakra System to better understand our surroundings. I see them working much like butterfly nets, scooping up information in our vicinity that then gets funneled to the Chakra System for analysis. The data gets translated and broadcasted for our use in the decision-making process in the hopes that the "choice maker" (the free will human being) moves in the direction that best supports the overall experience.

Let Me Paint a Picture

If a painter wanted to sit down in front of a beautiful landscape and put it to canvas, he might start with the broad strokes. Each one marking the shapes and landmarks, making sure to get the scale just right. Once he was satisfied with the overall size and placement, he would then come in with the fine strokes of color, shadow, highlights, and texture. This would bring the picture to life, allowing the full expression of the artist's intention.

The four bodies are much like the broad strokes to the painter. They scoop up the overall energies in our field. They gather up information on a large scale to help the human navigate their immediate experience. The four bodies then deliver the information to the Chakra System, which acts like the fine strokes to the artist.

The chakras filter and translate the collected data and report their findings to the conscious (and sometimes subconscious) human. This offers the appropriate information for the person to be able to navigate based on their emotions, intuitive hunches, gut instincts, and the overall "feel" of the situation. Step by step, you are building yourself to be the proactive human living with purpose. Exercising each layer of the four bodies strengthens the barometer that you innately are. When the chakras and four bodies work in harmony with each other, it is quite the work of art!

Nesting Dolls

Remember the Russian nesting dolls? Those cute wooden dolls that decreased in size so they would neatly rest within each other? Our Four Body System stacks exactly in the same manner. When we are anchored, connected, and clear our layers are perfectly stacked within each other. Without any effort or force, these bodies simply self-regulate and maintain their placement. Each one thrives on its own but perfectly supports the system as a whole.

When we experience long bouts of stress the four bodies can wobble out of their alignment. When we allow ourselves to be overworked, fatigued, or believe negating programs of fear and low worth, our layers misalign. Think of it like dropping a plate onto the floor, how it might roll around a few times before settling. When our bodies wobble this way for long periods of time we can experience the sensation of being unstable and discombobulated. We'll have more moments of clumsiness, where we drop things or stub our toes on furniture. There may even be a looming sense of chaos in our lives, even if we can't pinpoint the reason for that sensation. We lack clarity in our day-to-day decisions, and in response, our other systems begin to shut down, going into protection mode.

Layer by Layer

Let's take a look at what the auric field is comprised of, including the roles of each "body." First, a sexy visual aid:

4 BODY SYSTEM

"CELLULAR MEMBRANE"

PHYSICAL

EMOTIONAL

MENTAL

SPIRITUAL

Physical Body

The first layer, the closest to the body is called the physical (etheric) body. It is the tactile and responsive layer that kicks in the fight-or-flight mechanism when needed. Because this one is the densest of all the layers, this is where sensation, pain, discomfort, and pleasure ignites. Once the "cause" has reached this layer, it will affect the physical body in a tangible way. Our body will manifest evidence of the event through skin irritation, wounds, bruising, goosebumps, stomach aches, or anything of that nature.

Let's say, you're walking downtown at night and suddenly become hyper-aware that something isn't right. You are present to a feeling of dread down a certain street, and you just know you shouldn't go that way. Your aura is collecting data and delivering it to the root chakra, giving you the signal that you need to get to safety. This might manifest in the body as a stomach ache, shortness of breath, or a very tangible, heavy sense of dread. Once you are in the clear that feeling subsides.

Here's how that experience might look in the chakras and aura: The spiritual body (intuition) collected the data that something was wrong, sent it to the root for the alarm (safety/security), then to your physical body (stomach ache, chills, etc.) and emotional body (sense of dread) in the hopes that you would listen and choose another street. All of these components working together, delivering the message for your bodily safety.

This is also the layer that alerts us to our physical needs such as diet, hydration, intake of oxygen, and rest. It is where we take in sunlight, feel cool autumn breezes, and snuggle up with our favorite blanket when we've had a bad day. Basically, the physical body is where we nurture and support our physical body (redundant, I know). Without these sensations, we would neglect our needs, leaving the body weak and malnourished. And without a body, we have no life.

Emotional Body

Moving outward, the second layer is called the emotional (astral) body. This is where our emotional wisdom responds to our experiences. Empaths have a very thick and sensitive emotional body, which is why they get easily overwhelmed by crowded situations and public events. It is also why you can't ever lie to an Empath. They feel it, trapped in their emotional field like a bug on a windshield. Splat!

Empath or not, we all have emotions, and when we learn to honor and listen to them, they can be incredibly handy when navigating through life. Even the most emotionally closed person makes decisions based on how they feel from time to time. Haven't you ever been in a demeaning job or toxic relationship and just *knew* it was time to leave? The feeling was as real as it could be but you had no evidential proof. Your heart knew it was time to move away from that situation, and it was relaying that to you through your emotional body to the wisdom of your heart chakra. You felt it was just over. Did you listen and allow yourself to walk away? Or did you push down your emotions and continue on as if nothing was wrong? Often, we mistrust what our emotions are telling us and stay in unhealthy situations using logic and reason to justify our decisions. It's only in hindsight do we understand what our emotional body was telling us.

Our emotional body monitors our overall reactions to experiences, providing us the information to make decisions that will support our life. The key to working with this layer is to honor how you feel. I know that sounds overly simplified but there is an emotional disconnect of epidemic proportions on this planet. When we judge, condemn, or attack our feelings, we stuff them down and nullify them. Often, we hold onto the negative emotions, punishing ourselves for having them. And yet we strive for the happy ones, thinking that will make us happy. But how can we have one without the other? We cannot have only half of the totality. We are whole. We are emotional creatures. We carry ALL the emotions within our being. To play favorites with some is to judge the others as wrong.

Unfortunately, we live in a society where feelings have very little value. Especially for our men. They have been told their whole lives to "be a man" anytime they showed an ounce of emotion. Even going so far as being bullied for having a softer side and showing compassion towards others. People are programmed to believe that showing emotion is a weakness, leaving them disconnected to the very wisdom that resides there.

> **"God turns you from one feeling to another and teaches by means of opposites so that you will have two wings to fly, not one." - Rumi**

Maybe this has happened to you in the past. At some point, you realized you stuff down your feelings for fear of someone seeing them and judging you for having them. If so, perhaps the first step is to simply observe them and let them be whatever they want to be. Without judgment. Without condemnation. Simply observe yourself having whatever emotion is washing over you. Watch yourself wanting to shove it down, but perhaps this time you don't. You may just realize they don't hurt as much as you think they will. And before long you'll be tapping into the well of wisdom that is your Emotional Guidance System.

Mental Body

The third layer is the mental body. This is where thought, logic, and thought-based inspirations collect. We've heard many times how thoughts create. Well, this is where they begin to grow in power. Haven't you ever been stumped with a question or wondered what the next step in a project needed to be, only to suddenly have the answer? That inspiration came through your mental body. Your butterfly nets collected the data and delivered it to the chakra that would be able to translate the information – your crown and third eye chakras more than likely. It's how you were suddenly able to see/hear/feel/know the answer.

This is the layer that oversees our ability to maintain focus, awareness, and comprehension. It is the layer our Sacred Observer uses to deliver mind-expanding data down to the lower self in order to help with the decision-making process. The Sacred Observer is the part of us that can see the bigger picture and better understands the motives from which our free will selves choose our experience. It has the greater vantage point to witness whatever we are doing, as if another person is watching. We also access the higher mind from this layer, giving us the ability to think beyond our human comprehension. The trick is to not get swallowed up by the ego mind, or lower mind. That too, resides in the mental body. But like I've said, all aspects have a light and a shadow side. The mind is no different. (If this conversation has totally confused you, don't worry, I cover these concepts further down the road. Hang in there.)

Anytime we practice viewing our experience from the Sacred Observer, we are able to choose whether we want to listen to the higher mind or the lower mind. This ability provides the opportunity to choose things that will actually work for us and not just the temporary "fix" that provides false comfort. It's like having X-ray vision as your superpower. Only this kind of vision makes you aware of your motives and lets you know when you're being a bonehead!

> **"As you think, so shall you become."**
> **- Bruce Lee**

Spiritual Body

And finally, the fourth layer is the spiritual (causal) body. This is where we collect our spiritual guidance, inspiration, and connection from Source. It is the layer that allows us to connect to our guides, deceased loved ones, and into any other magickal realm we wish to delve. This layer is the least dense of the four, so it has the easiest time retrieving information from non-physical beings such as spirit guides and angels. (Don't let it get weird. Stay with me.)

I truly believe we are all capable of receiving and understanding psychic/intuitive information. It simply depends on the openness and willingness of the person and practicing the style in which one receives that information. Even if you don't believe you are capable of having these abilities, haven't you ever just KNOWN something? Without any proof or evidence, something was unequivocally true or you knew instantly it was false. You see a vision in your mind, someone calls right when you think of them, you abruptly stop just before getting into an accident…these are all intuitive based experiences. We are all connected to the wisdom available. Some just work to open it further, that's all. But it is there. Within all of us.

The spiritual body is the layer in which we commit ourselves to making the changes we want in our lives. There must first be the desire to change in order for us to take action towards those changes. Hermetic teachings state, "As above, so below, as within, so without, as the universe, so the soul…" This means that if we want our outer world to be XYZ, we must take the necessary steps in our inner world to reflect those desires. We must *be* what we want to have.

If we want to receive love in our lives we must be that love from within. "As within, so without" states in order to have what we want in our external world we must be its match internally, first. It's only in being it will we be capable of having it come to us. If we don't inwardly match our outward desire, we simply will not allow it into our lives.

Ask anyone who was ever offered an amazing promotion at work or found the love of their life but didn't feel they deserved it. Without the belief that they truly deserved what was being offered, more than likely they rejected the offer and disallowed it into their lives.

Four Glasses

There is another valuable role our Four Body System plays in our life, one that monitors our overall health and wellness. If we wish to be spiritually connected, healthy, and thriving, then the physical, emotional, and mental states are equally important to nurture. These layers have their own directives but support each other as a whole. If one body is out of balance then the whole system will wobble.

Let's face it, most of us are overworked, underappreciated, and often driven to a breaking point trying to cater to everyone's needs within our circle. We want so badly to be loved and accepted that we rarely check in and honor our own energy levels. We worry what people think of us, how they judge us, and if they'll like us. That steers our decision-making process to choose things that don't necessarily support true health and vitality. If we don't check in with our energy levels on a regular basis this "vehicle" will be in serious need of repair. So again, it is up to us to keep an eye on our systems and make sure they are all working smoothly.

One of the visuals I use quite often is that of four glasses of water. Imagine them sitting on a table in front of you, each one representing one layer of your four bodies: physical, emotional, mental, and spiritual. The goal is to manage their "fullness" in order to keep them balanced and hydrated. In our crazy-tunnel-vision-blowing-and-going lifestyle we tend to be obsessed with one area of life while neglecting the others. This leaves the remaining glasses dried up and crusty.

There are times in my life when I feel Spirit is downloading my higher mind with new information, and I have to get it down on paper (or screen) before I forget it. I might be in front of the computer 10-12 hours a day, for two or three days in a row. I can't help it. The words are just pouring out of me. I have surrendered at that point to being the vessel, happily allowing Spirit to speak through me. In those moments, my spiritual and mental bodies are the ones being activated.

If I let that process go on for too many days the inactive layers (physical and emotional) will begin to suffer. My body begins to ache from lack of circulation and mobility. My back, shoulders, and hip flexors will be tight from sitting at the computer all day. And at times when I've really pushed myself too hard, I'll get emotionally overwhelmed and extremely sensitive. It would be very important at that point for me to take a break, "fill those other glasses up," and bring myself back into balance. Going for a walk, doing some yoga, watching a fun movie, or going to a comedy club are great examples of ways to fill up the physical and emotional glasses.

Or let's say I've been organizing and decluttering the garage and the summer heat and physical exertion is starting to deplete my body. Not to mention the emotional drain of throwing things out that I am emotionally attached to. Maybe something as simple as taking a break for meditation or playing a little Sudoku would satisfy the system to come back into balance.

In my case, since I work every minute of every day in the spiritual conversation with clients, classes, radio, and casual conversation, if I don't go for a walk from time to time, I can feel my bodies wobble a bit and get out of alignment. Basically, my nesting dolls are not fitting together so well anymore, and they need a little adjusting. It's my responsibility to do whatever is needed to stack them properly again.

Have you ever played with a hula hoop by spinning it like a top? Once it slows down, it wobbles for a moment before settling on the ground. When we are overworked, underbalanced, and struggling to find our center, this is precisely the way our four bodies behave. Grounding and centering are definitely the first steps to bring them back into alignment, but it could take further proactive steps on your part to fully integrate. Tuning in from time to time, looking at the activities that have been capturing your attention, and making small (sometimes large) adjustments can help. If we give too much attention, energy, effort, and/or exertion to one layer while ignoring the others, the whole system will eventually break down.

The goal really is to check in a few times a week. Know yourself inside and out, what supports you, and wants diminishes your vitality. Create a true intimate relationship with your own energetic bodies. What enlivens you? What depletes you? When you have a stronger awareness of your whole self, you'll be able to easily identify when you've lost your center as well as to know what will bring you back into alignment. Pay attention to your behavior and what is drawing your attention at the moment. If you feel off, look at what you've been doing the past few days that may have caused you to wobble. Have you just simply exhausted one of the bodies and the others could use a little attention? Sometimes, it's as simple as that. At other times, they require major life changes in various activities, diet, or stress levels. Give yourself what you need to fill up those glasses and see if that equalizes and centers you.

Boomerang

There's a chance you've heard the Law of Attraction (LOA) lingo of "putting it out there?" Well, there is a reason that's a thing. Putting something "out there" means to send a request off into the ethers and have it return as an actualized "thing." That request can be a conscious or unconscious act. We're basically writing a newspaper ad to the Universe with our request in the hopes that it answers us back.

Radiate

The action of sending our request first passes through our physical body with focused intent and kinetic energy. We build up our energy, take the necessary steps, put our affairs in order, and do what needs to be done to receive the thing we want. There are many times we send intentions out into space mindlessly, which is why we have experiences that we didn't really want but somehow know we had a hand in. We are creation beings, after all. And the sooner we accept the responsibility of that, the better off we'll be.

After our physical layer does its part, the request then mixes with our emotional and mental bodies. This fuels the intention with passion and excitement, giving it a bit of "oomph." I call that our jet fuel and the rocket can't take off without it. The thoughts and emotions are important to launch the request with precision. If we overthink the process or feel emotionally incapable of handling such a request, our rocket won't get off the ground. Or worse, it will shoot off into another direction. All three elements must align – physical action, emotional acceptance, and unattached mental focus – in order for the request to launch properly.

I've heard it said that the Universe answers us every time. No matter the question, it always responds. Which is why it's doubly important to watch what you are thinking and how you feel about the ad you are placing in the paper. (Yeah, I changed metaphors on you, go with it.) If you really want it but secretly don't feel like you deserve it, there is a conflict in your request. Or, you really believe you can have it but you don't want it because of all the added stress that "thing" might cause in your life. Again, that's contradictory to what you are asking for. The answer you get back might be a little confusing because the Universe sees the conflict in your request and sends back its best guess.

But, let's say you really want it, your emotions and thoughts are equally aligned with your desire, and you are willing to receive with open arms upon its return. Finally, your intention reaches the spiritual body where it is charged with inspiration, guidance, stardust, and wonder. We daydream about its arrival. We marvel at the process of magickal manifestation. And we anticipate what it will be like once it's here.

Memory Lane: A few years ago, I was visiting a friend in Salt Lake City and for fun we decided to go to an amusement park in the area. We both loved roller coasters so obviously that was our first choice of rides. As we waited in line she turned to me and asked if I had a preference of seating. Calmly, I said it didn't really matter, as long as it was either the first seat or the last. But NOT the middle! When I said it, I put so much emphasis on the middle section, even to the point of feeling a bit of anger towards the possibility of being seated there. Sure enough, as the people from the previous ride exited the seats and we were shuffled into the lanes, we were placed in the very middle seat of the coaster. We both just looked at each other in amazement and burst into laughter. The Universe didn't register my calm request for the front or back. But it sure heard my loud request for the middle. How could it not? That's where I put all my energy. And as they say, the Universe doesn't differentiate between what you want and don't want. It only registers where your attention goes. Lesson learned.

Reaching the end of your spiritual body, the request has left your field. There is no more to do on your end. It is quite literally out of your hands at that point. You've done all you can do. Now just let it go and trust that it will return in the perfect timing and in the fashion that serves your Highest Good. (Notice I said perfect timing...you can't control when it comes back any more than you can control how it comes back.)

Imagine tossing a baseball straight up into the air. There are three significant steps:

1. Effort is required on your part to provide the propulsion to launch the ball.
2. In the air, the ball reaches its peak and pauses for a brief moment.
3. It then returns whence it came.

This is how I see LOA working. We are responsible for the initial send-off: the energy that propels the ball upward. But once it leaves our space, we have nothing left to do but await its return and "catch it" when it comes back.

This is a 2-part process that can be difficult for some.

1. We stress about whether or not it will come back. We fret over whether or not we did everything correctly. And we worry we might not succeed in our efforts. That ignites our control-freak within, tempting us to micromanage the process. Humans have a general issue with letting things go. This is one of those instances.
2. When we have evidence that our work is coming to fruition we freak out over the fact that we did it correctly. For some reason we fear success. We might feel unworthy of it being in our life. We could worry about the added stress this new found success will bring. Or we attach to how people will view us once we have this gift in our lives. All of that makes us want to move out of the way and not catch the ball when it is coming back down.

Once the request boomerangs back towards you, it lands in your spiritual body as either intuitive confirmation, validation from your guides, or as a sort of "ah-ha" inspirational moment. This is the point in time where you might see little clues that look a lot like your request but aren't quite fully actualized. These inspired moments are letting us know that what we've asked for is on its way. I call these "spiritual winks" as if to say the Universe acknowledges my request and is letting me know the message was received and all is well.

But if for some reason you are getting feedback that isn't looking like how you intended, it's the perfect time to make small adjustments in your intention. That's usually when I'll meditate a bit, looking for any resistance, fear, stress, or worry on my end. It gives me the opportunity to clean up the energy so that I'm more open to receive and I'm not secretly trying to sabotage my efforts. It's important to not get overly attached or have any expectations at this point, just enjoy the clues as they drop in front of you and make adjustments as needed.

Eventually, it reaches our mental body, giving us inspired thoughts and perhaps dreams about its arrival. We might even have some insights on things we need to do in preparation for it. Soon-to-be-mothers know this feeling very well. This is when they get a strong urge to nest. Their wisdom is saying, "The baby will be here soon so you need to get ready."

When what we've asked for passes through the emotional body, we feel a bit of excitement, knowing that what we have intended is coming. We may have some clarity that we're on the right track because of the feelings we have about whatever is showing up. Often this is where we tend to sabotage our process because we freak out at the realization that we might actually succeed. Humans for some reason fear success just as much, if not more than failure. It's quite the interesting phenomenon.

Once it hits our physical body, it has materialized into form. It is showing up as physical evidence in response to our request. This is how we birth what is within us, transforming thoughts, wishes, and desires into actualized tangible experiences. Something to keep in mind though, it doesn't always show up the way you intended. This would be a great time to not attach to the outcome, accept what arrives, and try again if you wish.

To have this process run smoothly, you must align yourself with your request. As within, so without. Double check to see if you're nervous about what you've asked for. Many times we say we want it, but secretly (or even subconsciously) we are afraid of it actually happening. Or other times, we get so attached to wanting it the way we want it that we are stressed out and feel disappointed when it doesn't return in that form. And yes, given that we tend to have low self-worth, we'll even harbor a belief that we don't deserve the thing we're dreaming of.

Anytime I'm working with this LOA process and I've stated my intent, I finish it off with a mantra "this or something better" at the end. Adding that little flourish is me saying to the Universe "I want what I'm asking for and I'm going to work towards that outcome. But if you see something that would be better for me, I'm open to that as well." For me, it magickally takes off the pressure to perfectly succeed and it relaxes my energy so that I can indeed receive whatever returns. By saying that mantra, I am affirming "I want what I want but I'm open to what's best." Which is exactly the perfect mix when creating for your Highest Good.

Tennis Anyone?

My Guys gave me the perfect metaphor to help illustrate the way this giving-receiving-letting-go-of-attachment game works. Imagine you are on a tennis court and playing the Universe (or your Guidance Team, either works, depending on your needs). You are in charge of your half of the court. They are in charge of the other half. The net marks the center, perfectly dividing the court 50/50. You are responsible for 100% of your half. That is it. Anything on that half is yours. How you play the game is all on you. What you wear, the racket you use, and whether or not you wear your hair in pigtails. All you. But that is it. You have no say in what happens on the other side of that net. This can feel like a good thing or a bad thing, depending on the level of control one needs to feel safe. Control freaks will want to reject the thought. But to me, there is peace in that math. It means I don't have to do everything and that I am supported in life.

When you send out a request, you serve the ball. All the hard work, practice, and self-care has prepared you for this moment as you steady yourself, focus, and aim. In life, it means there are mundane steps to take to create new experiences. If you're looking for a new job, you must put your resume out into the world. If you want to be an artist, you'll need to sign up for some classes and buy art supplies. There is a level of accountability on your part to have the things you want. It's not going to magickally fall into your lap. When the ball soars over the net, it is now out of your hands. You have done everything you can at that point.

When the Universe hits the ball back, this can look like further guidance or inspiration to support your endeavor. By hitting it back to them, you are indicating that you are following through with their suggestions. It comes back with more evidence, you hit back to say "thank you" and they hit again with "you're welcome." And now you have a game. If you were to serve the ball, jump over the net to hit back from their side, then back over to hit from your side and so on, you are working really hard to control the whole process. You are stating to the Infinite Cosmos that you do not trust it'll get done. This dominating message you are broadcasting is fear based, lacks faith, and is attached to being right. In essence, you are acting from your shadow ego by trying to control the entire picture.

We are not required to run the whole game. We are invited to work in concert with the Universe. To take ownership for our part of the deal, but also trust that they've got the rest covered. When we micromanage all the elements, we exhaust ourselves. It's hard jumping over that net constantly, trying to control a situation that isn't ours to control. And who's to say we know what we're doing anyway? What if what they want to send back to us is a million times better than what we requested? But we're too busy demanding it come to us the way we are attached to. So very limiting!

How they hit it back is not up to you. *If* they hit it back isn't up to you, either. That is the moment when you must let go of the outcome, believe that you've done all you can do, and trust. This is when I speak about Highest Good. What comes back to you may not always look the way you thought it would. The Universe, angels and guides, and any other spiritual support system you have with you are all diligently working to provide the experiences that will best serve you. Sometimes, that means the ball comes back unrecognizable, but it is for you, nonetheless. Please know too, the Highest Good doesn't always look pretty. It isn't always going to be the easiest route or the gentlest journey. Sometimes, it means falling flat on your face in order to learn a valuable lesson. And that lesson you learned could play a valuable role in the next game of tennis that you actually win.

I'm not about to claim that I am an expert on manifestation and the LOA. I, too, am just scratching the surface of this gigantic conversation. In fact, most humans are not aware of the power that resides within them. We limit ourselves on a daily basis without even a thought of the magnitude that is within us. Silly humans.

But know this, you are a powerful creator, capable of sculpting your life into a work of art. And the good news is you don't have to do it all by yourself. Sometimes, life can feel that way though. As we dodge the bullets and deflect the daggers. Some days we wonder why we're even here. What's the point? Right? But, there is a whole, vast Universe just waiting to support your dreams and desires. You have an army of sacred, eternal beings on your side, ready to ride this ride with you. All I'm attempting to do is to pull back the curtain for you a little bit and give you a peek to what could be. Just to give you a taste of the limitless possibilities that's within you. It's up to you to rip the curtain all the way open and see for yourself. Do you dare?

CHAPTER 6

$\mathcal{R}$eceive

If you're still with me, I just want to say thanks for staying open-minded and being willing to explore these conversations. It's not always easy hearing new information. Especially, if it makes you question the entire construct in which you live. It seems the more we dig, the more we uncover our shadow. The more shadow we see the more we feel naked and exposed. But remember what I said before: That is where all the best nutrition resides.

So onward we go!

To You or *For* You?

Many of us feel like life is happening *to* us. We run around, get in the game, buy and consume, hurry up and wait, and try not to die. So much fear based, reactionary living. It's exhausting! I don't think we're necessarily born that way, though. I'd like to think that we have an innate sense of optimism when we enter this world. Over time however, life seems to beat us down, robbing us of the infinite joy this world holds. It domesticates our free spirit and creates generations of moldable, compliant humans. We sit still with our little hands in our laps, doing what we're told, playing our roles, and just waiting until something happens to us. Then we spring into action, deciphering whether or not we are in danger, and react in the way that will lead us to safety. I'm not sure if you feel this way, but to me that is not what I'm going for in life.

I'm of the thinking that life is *for* us. It's happening so that we can be involved. So we can have adventures, change courses, take roads less traveled, and jump into the deep end of the pool. We are here for the whole dang experience. The messy, the lovely, the horrid, and the inspired. Yes, things come towards us, sometimes unpleasant things. But we have more power than we give ourselves credit for.

In the previous chapters, I've talked a lot about various systems, spiritual versus physical energies, and how we can collect data to help us navigate the ins and outs of human life. Going forward, we'll put all those systems to work and discuss the human in action. For a moment, if you don't mind, let's review all we've covered thus far.

THE SYSTEMS

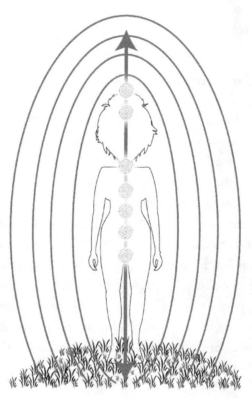

This picture is you. It's me. It's all humans regardless of race, gender, religion, sexual orientation, political affiliation, favorite color, or whatever you had for lunch. It's simply a human, comprised of a group of systems to assist navigation in the journey called life. And perhaps, you weren't aware of its entirety until now, but trust me, everyone looks like this energetically. Consider it part of your package deal as you were moving through the birth canal. Yay!

The grounding and centering connection acts like a lightning rod, anchoring you in the ground below and drawing spiritual energy in from above. The chakras are lined up on that rod, much like a string of pearls, balanced, ignited, and aligned. We then move outwardly to the Four Body System, where it is stacked ever so neatly in its perfect placement, housing you in the prettiest bubble ever. The outer layer of the spiritual body is what I call the "cellular membrane," just to make the point that everything inside of it is our container of personal power. There are other teachings that talk of more layers from that point, and I'm not discrediting them, but for this conversation we're only focusing on these four layers (physical, emotional, mental, and spiritual).

Everything within that membrane is yours! Your power resides in that delicious bubble of existence. The words you speak, your thoughts and emotions, the choices you make, and the action you put to those choices…YOU. All you. That is your power. That is the only part of the entire Universe you are in charge of. That is your side of the tennis court. And yes, this is the point where many of us become control freaks because that's a hard pill to swallow, knowing that is the limit of our personal power. But the truth remains. It is so.

If you were to go just one single inch outside of that cellular membrane, you would be in the external world. You have no power over the events outside of your personal space. You cannot control another person's free will, even though some often try through manipulation and coercion. You cannot impose your will in the hopes that things play out the way you want. You can't force or push things to your liking. Oh, we try. Believe me! We would all like to think that we have control over those things. We spend so much energy pushing and pulling, crafting our external experience only to realize the truth in the end. That it was never ours to control.

When we align ourselves, retracting all of the energy we expend trying to control our environment, we begin to understand that we are indeed powerful beings. That energy pools up within our bubble, filling us with vitality and life force. Our power is better served within our own space, rather than spraying it all over in the hopes that we will be able to control the outcome. Pushing your will outside of your space is exhausting. If you were to collect it, bring it back, and focus it where it is belongs, you would have more stamina for your own endeavors. All because you have chosen to focus inward and apply your power appropriately. Within you!

Let's Be Clear Here

I've lightly touched on this conversation before, but now it's time to really throw it out on the table and get messy with it. We are all psychic. We are all intuitive. Every single person on the planet has the ability to read, pick up, collect, and comprehend the unseen, unknown, and incomprehensible information available in the ethers. Every single person. That means you, too. (Just in case you're over there thinking I'm wrong about you.) We each have our own styles of reading that information, but make no mistake about it, we are all gifted in the ways of intuition.

Remember the butterfly nets? They are collecting data every second of our life. Our eyes, ears, and brains are constantly inundated with information from every direction. Our brains are processing so much information that we are not conscious of it all. It files away in our subconscious and unconscious libraries as "junk mail" so to not

106

overwhelm our conscious mind. And that's just the everyday mundane stuff.

Now expand your mind even more and look at the possibility that you are also collecting data beyond what is in the physical realm. Your nets are gathering the subtle information as well. Sometimes, it's fantastical. Sometimes, a little spooky. But trust me when I say, we all do it. It is simply a natural occurrence.

There are many that practice these skills, affording them the ability to help others by relaying intuitive information. Much like a bodybuilder might strengthen his muscles before entering into a competition, psychics and mediums practice and strengthen their intuitive muscles so to be able to use them with greater accuracy.

As the nets gather up these subtle bits of data, they pass through what is called the clairs. Working in harmony with specific chakras, these clairs are where psychic information gets collected and translated to be relayed and used as guidance, insight, and knowledge. Whether we are aware of it or not, we make decisions all the time from our gut instincts, hunches, and feelings. Call it what you want, but this is intuition in action.

Born This Way

We are all born with the clairs intact, even though we may not be aware that we're using them. The type of childhood trauma we experienced, how much our caregivers supported our intuition, and our socio-economic upbringing will determine how healthy our clairs are throughout our lives. Anytime we are teased, bullied, or abused for having imaginary friends, seeing ghosts, or just random musings of childhood fantasy, we will shut these channels down in order to be normal and stay safe. Essentially, we become domesticated to survive the harshness of the world.

It is true though, we are born the way we are born. We each have our own style of intuition, our own magick to share with the world. They may be dormant but with a little acknowledgment, a smidge of practice, and a touch of trust, you can start using these little babies alongside your other innate systems.

As you read through each clair, you may see yourself in one or more of the descriptions. That's perfectly natural. Or you may not relate at all but can still see possibilities here and there. I would suggest not trying to make anything fit right now. Putting yourself into a box limits your possibilities and stifles the expansive being that you are. On the other side of the coin, I also suggest that you not immediately reject the ideas offered because you can't see the traits within you. Just read it, roll around in it, and whatever resonates keep it in your pocket. Whatever doesn't resonate, just set it aside. (I'd say throw it out but you might find yourself returning to it somewhere down the road.) Take it slow, stay open, and see where you end up when the dust settles.

There are generally two ways we receive clair information. We can experience it physically as in a tangible/mundane kind of way (road signs, street signs, license plates, etc.). Or we get it spiritually, meaning it's "not of this world" or invisible to others. Guides are extremely creative, as I'm sure you'll see if you decide to work with them.

Memory Lane: Back in the day, when I was working very hard at pretending to be normal, I started getting the sense that angels were trying to get my attention. They would whisper in my ear, tap me on the shoulder, and give me visions in the hopes that I would be open to a relationship. At that time, however, I wasn't interested in the least. I was under the impression that they were going to judge me for not living a certain way, and I just didn't want to hear it. So, I kept pushing them away, telling them to leave me alone.

They probably knew the only way to get through to me was to be covert about it and not let me know it was them. Stealthy little buggers! They began putting things in front of me to get my attention but not in a way that was obviously them. This was right around the time in my life when I was a new mother and had just started working for an all-women's gym in Tucson. In the locker room, we had a cork board where people could share their business cards, flyers, and special announcements. One day, I was perusing the postings when I saw a card that interested me. I don't remember what it was but it had nothing to do with angels. I reached up to grab it, thought to myself I would write the lady's number down, and then put the card back for someone else. As I pulled the thumbtack out, a second card fell to the ground and I heard "That card is for you." And wouldn't you know it, it said, "Angel Readings."

Needless to say, I laughed a little, gave in a bit, and called her. I joined her classes and learned as much as possible. I finally stopped resisting, remained open-minded, and my life has never been the same since. Thank goodness for their persistence and clever ways.

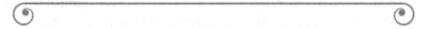

Even though there are several clairs we could cover, I want to take you through the main four. As we walk through them, I invite you to see where you might have the traits discussed in each one. Try to keep in mind, these are suggestions and jumping off points. We're not wanting to immediately put you in a box. Simply try them on for size and see what fits.

To the Clairs!

CLAIRVOYANT
Clear Seeing – Third Eye Chakra

Having this psychic sense in your repertoire means your third eye has the ability to see things that not everyone sees. There are variations of how one might have these visions. It all depends on the person, their openness, and their innate gift. But in general, it means having the capability to receive messages on a visual level.

Clairvoyants can have prophetic dreams, giving them pertinent information about themselves, a close friend or relative, or even a larger event involving an area of the world. While awake, they can sometimes have visions, much like a movie playing in their mind. Sometimes, visions can be about past events, the future, or even a warning about something in the present tense. My Guys understand my love for movies and certain television series. Because of this, they use my favorite scenes to convey specific messages to me. I'll see the scene in my mind and will know instantly what they are trying to tell me. That's the beautiful thing about our guides, they know our language and are more than happy to speak to us in a way that we'll understand.

Some clairvoyants can see angels, spirits, or other spiritual beings with their physical eyes. They are standing right in front of them and can clearly see them just as they would see you and me. Sometimes, though, their vision is more internal, within their mind's eye. That is when the clairvoyant can picture them standing there in their mind but don't actually see them with their physical eyes. It's gets a little confusing sometimes because we wonder if it's just our imagination. We humans love our proof, so when there is no physical evidence (like someone standing right in front of us), we typically just push the vision aside and ignore it.

Until you figure out how your own third eye works, I suggest staying open and remain patient. It takes practice but eventually your chakra will balance, regulate, and expand, allowing your inner vision to become a strong ally in your life. I used to get so frustrated because I typically don't see with my physical eyes. It's always in my mind's eye. But I really, Really, *REALLY* wanted to see. I mean, who doesn't want all the bells and whistles, right? But having a strong attachment caused frustration. And with frustration, came judgment and anger. With anger came irritation in the chakra. Therefore, my vision started to close down. (I sounded like Yoda a little bit there.) Once I let go of my own expectations and honored the way I was built, my chakra relaxed, and I could see again. Honestly, ever since I accepted who I was and let go of my judgment, my sight has come in stronger. The moral of the story? You can't force this stuff. You are who you are. Learn to work with it rather than force it to be something it isn't.

On a mundane level, our guides are amazingly creative when offering guidance. Clairvoyants will get messages in the form of billboards, license plates, road signs, and any other tangible thing that lands in front of us to get our attention. Sometimes, we either don't trust our psychic vision, aren't aware of it, or just plain distracted with life in general. So when our guides are really wanting to get our attention, they will fashion some sort of message in physical form. That way it is hard to miss and hopefully causes us to stop for a bit and pay attention.

Memory Lane: I remember once while living in Boise, I was feeling pretty disjointed in life. While driving to teach an angel class, I was talking out loud to my Guys, asking them to help me understand where I belonged. And I didn't mean it so much about the geography, more of an existential kind of pondering. I didn't feel like I was on the right path or making a difference in my work. I felt pretty lost and overwhelmed. Just then, a car with the license plate UR HOME drove up next to me, changed lanes to get in front of me, and then rode along with me for a few miles until my turn. In that moment, I realized they were saying "It's okay. You are home, and you're doing great." Needless to say, I started crying, and my makeup was a mess for the class. But I had a great story to share with them about angels.

I've noticed too, that clairvoyants tend to be visual lovers in general. They seem to be drawn to careers where color and flow are the focus. Art, interior design, fashion, photography, landscaping, and architecture are all tantalizing careers to a clairvoyant. Even if they are unaware that that's the reason why. They crave the kind of nutrition that only their eyes can provide. For them, things must be beautiful, well lit, and soothing to their soul in whatever medium that speaks to their creative side.

It's important to note that if you feel you have this gift, be sure to give yourself "visual downtime." Create a soothing sanctuary where you can rest your eyes. Dim the lights, light a few candles, and give your eyes a rest. This will allow your third eye to recharge and clear from the day's stimulation.

CLAIRAUDIENT
Clear Hearing – Ear Chakras

Remember when we discussed the chakras, and I mentioned why I like including the ear chakras? Well, this is the reason why. Being clairaudient means you have the ability to hear sounds, voices, and messages that others might not be privy to. Again, those messages can be spiritual, or they can be mundane.

Like my clairvoyance, I don't hear with my physical ears very often. I typically hear the voices inside my head, and that can be just as confusing as it sounds. It took me a few years to understand that I wasn't talking to myself, that I was actually receiving guidance. It's tricky too, because we talk to ourselves all the damn time! So, now throw in a few more voices, and it can crowded in the head very quickly. I learned a little trick though, to help me distinguish my voice from theirs. I listen for the pronouns. When I hear "I need to do that" or "I shouldn't have done that," right away, I get that I'm talking to myself.

Also note that if it's in a judgmental tone, it's probably just your inner critic scolding you. Guides don't talk like that to us. They aren't in it to judge and condemn us for our choices. They simply want to guide and support us so their messages are never about criticism or shame. When I hear things like "we'd like for you to..." or "we suggest that you go..." I know it's them. Guides will always love you no matter what you choose. They just want to nudge in the direction that works best for you.

Remember, we all have free will and can say no at any time. Which is why they offer suggestions instead of dictating what they think we should or shouldn't do. They're not in the judgment game like we humans are. They've got better things to do than to make us feel ashamed for whatever we think we're doing wrong.

Another aspect of spiritual hearing is sometimes the clairaudient will hear songs, music, or tones inside their head and/or ears. I know sometimes I get a song stuck in my head, but that isn't necessarily what I'm talking about here. Have you ever heard a song right around the time you were waking up? And maybe you hadn't thought of that particular song in years. Or maybe it's just one line from a song but it keeps repeating. When this happens to me, I will go look up the lyrics and then listen to it online. It's usually my Guys giving me a message, again, in a way that I'm going to understand.

In the mundane world, clairaudients might hear a specific song on the radio right when they needed to hear it. Something that gives them the message that they are doing just fine on a particularly difficult day. Sirens, alarms, bells, and horns are sometimes used by our guides to get us to pay closer attention in that moment.

Guides will also use other people to deliver messages if the occasion should arise. Let's say you are walking by a group of people who are enjoying lunch and talking amongst themselves. Just as you pass by, one of them says something that hits you like a ton of bricks. That one sentence…boom! You needed to hear that very thing at that very moment. And yet, they are so involved in their conversation that they hardly notice you walking by. Your guides, in their infinite wisdom and unlimited creativity, took that opportunity to give you a message through another human. I don't know how they do it but it is super cool when it happens.

Gypsy Story: In 2011, I had been getting messages telling me that I was going to be taking a trip. Typically, this kind of guidance was fine. But the more they shared about it, the more I realized this was no regular trip. This is how the conversation went down:

Guys: We want you to start driving.
Me: Where am I going?
Guys: You'll see.
Me: How long will I be gone?
Guys: We can't be sure.
Me: How will I be paying for this trip?
Guys: Please just trust. Go.

They started calling it my gypsy trip, I think to entice me, sneaky bastards. For weeks I tried to avoid it, but they wouldn't have it. They were relentless about it. I would wake up in the middle of the night having a panic attack because of the weight of what they were asking me to do. I mean, come on! I was Control Freak Central! And here they are asking me to...just...drive?!

One fateful morning, upon waking from a deep sleep, I heard my boyfriend talking to my son about cleaning his room. He said, "You know what you need to do. Now, do it." I knew right then and there, that sentence was for me. It hit me so hard with truth, echoing in the house, booming with clarity. I had been putting it off because I was afraid, and they were saying I needed to jump. Guides are very clever, aren't they?

Clairaudient people crave sounds that they resonate with, so obviously they will gravitate towards careers that provide such things. Music, orchestras (whether playing an instrument or becoming a conductor), film score composers, meditation music producers, sound guys on Broadway, anything you could possibly think of that would involve sound, vibration, rhythm, and tone. Life *is* music and harmony. Clairaudients crave vibration and sound.

And just as our psychic seeing friends, if you feel you resonate with this group, then make sure you have plenty of downtime as well. Surround yourself with soothing music, water fountains, and try to keep away from sharp, disjointed noise. You might even need silence, nature sounds, or binary meditations to bring you into balance with your ear chakras. Give yourself anything that allows your ears to recharge and rest.

CLAIRSENTIENT
Clear Feeling – Heart Chakra

If you find yourself feeling drained each time you hang out with certain people, tend to get easily overwhelmed in large crowds and at public events, or have been known to cry at the drop of a hat at a cute baby commercial…you might be a clairsentient.

Another term for these beautifully sensitive creatures is Empath. And yes, all humans are capable of feeling empathy and having emotions, but it's not the same as being an Empath. They feel EVERYTHING. All the time. No matter what. And that can be very difficult, especially if you aren't aware that you are a member of this group.

Empaths have been coined the psychic sponges of the world because they walk around all day long just sucking up their environments. Most of the time, they are unaware that they are doing it. Quite often they do so to the point of causing health issues including chronic fatigue, adrenal and thyroid imbalances, and other ailments. It's quite the conundrum. To feel everything, but not absorb it. To remain an open vessel but not be overwhelmed by it. To be their fullest expression of love, but with healthy boundaries. That's the path of the Empath. The hero's journey so to speak.

When an Empath spends their day sucking up everyone else's emotions and energies, they tend to lose their own self-awareness. They are so bogged down with things that don't belong to them that it's difficult to find their way out of the mess. Without realizing it, they have clogged up their own navigation system, screwing up their natural barometer. They've lost their center. Over time, the weight of those energies gets to be too much for them to cope with so they might turn to external vices such as food or alcohol to help numb the discomfort. It becomes a lifelong attempt to just get through life.

One of my goals is to educate and empower as many Empaths as I can come into contact with. There's already a lot of chaos in the world, but for clairsentients, it can sometimes be unbearable to deal with. It requires a lot of practice, a ton of patience, and a bit of time to master boundaries. If you find yourself feeling like you belong to this group, have faith. Being born this way doesn't mean you simply have to deal with it. You can hone your craft, strengthen your tools, and make it work *for* you rather than have it *work you*.

Messages come in a variety of ways for Empaths. Because clairsentience works through the heart chakra, there is typically an emotional response to the situation at hand. They can walk into a room full of people and "read the vibe," allowing them to steer clear of groups they may not want to mingle with. They are capable of feeling the emotions of someone they're talking to, even if that person is putting on a good face. Even when asked if everything is alright, and they swear they are okay, an Empath knows better.

Being able to pick up emotions isn't just in the living world. Empaths could also be feeling a deceased human's emotions if they are in their immediate vicinity. When people die, there is a period of time where they are still very connected to their thoughts, emotions, and personality. Just because they have left their physical body behind doesn't mean you can't feel the rest of them. Especially if they are distressed or fearful of their current situation. You feel them when near because they are emitting their emotions in a sense to ask for help. Then there are other times of course, when they are very much at peace, and they just want to let someone know everything is okay as they go about their way.

I believe that inanimate objects can also store residual emotional energy. Areas of great devastation, land rich with history where wars have been fought, prisons and mental institutions from the turn of the century, even places where monuments are erected to honor the fallen. These areas can collect the emotions of the deceased as well as the mourners that gather to honor the dead. The organic materials in that area collect the residual emotions of not only those that passed but of each person that comes to pay their respects. As the Empath walks towards that area, they will feel whatever has collected there over time.

Gypsy Story: Once I took a little jaunt to Oklahoma City to stave off the cravings of a gypsy needing to drive. I had never been and again, I just trusted and drove. I have always loved the energy of a big city's downtown area, so I decided to park, take my camera and walk around. I soaked up the urban landscape, historical architecture, and awesome people watching. At one point I came around a corner and walked up onto a long chain link fence with various articles of memorabilia attached to it. Flowers, trinkets, number badges people used in races…so many things. At first I wasn't sure what it was. But then the waves of sadness hit me. I immediately started crying. The more I walked down the street, the more I cried. Two blocks worth of honoring the dead in a beautiful collage of memorabilia was a bit more than I was prepared for.

And then I realized, this was a memorial for the victims of the Oklahoma City bombing that took place on April 19, 1995. The emotions hit me like a ton of bricks. My empathic self was wide open because I was excited to see a new town, but then it just scooped up all that energy and sucked it in before I realized it. I needed to walk back around the corner, breathe a little, ground myself, and reset. Going into places like this wasn't uncommon for me, but I wasn't prepared for it. After a few moments of collecting myself and setting up my boundaries, I was able to spend most of the afternoon walking around, being present with the memorial, and honoring those that were lost that day.

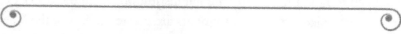

Receive

Please don't get me wrong, I know it sounds like being an Empath is somewhat of a curse. But it truly isn't. It's my favorite superpower of all. I feel the truth. I can tell when I'm being lied to, whether someone is listening to me or when their thoughts have wandered off. My favorite moment is when I'm giving a reading and it's difficult for them to receive what I'm saying because I've pushed a button or two. I can tell when they understand and agree with what I'm saying and when they are angry and think I'm full of it.

Really when you think about it, it goes much deeper than just being able to read the emotions of our surroundings. We are deciphering vibration. We are drawing in the vibrational frequencies of what is around us and translating it into knowable, usable information. Then, we have the ability to adjust our coordinates if we are headed into an environment that just isn't going to work for us. It is the ultimate barometer!

For clairsentients, the connection to their own emotions is crucial. In order to distinguish if they are picking up someone else's emotions, they need to have a closer relationship with their own. Sadly, however, as children they are often teased for being too sensitive, too emotional, and called crybabies. Years of experiencing shame for their innate gift has lead them to push down their feelings and second guess their own guidance. As adults, they have learned to put their emotions last for fear of being called out by their peers. This leaves the Empath to live a life disconnected from their own beautiful gift and eventually loss of trust with themselves.

Part of the patience I mentioned before is the journey back to trusting yourself and listening to that intuitive hit when you feel something, to not just put it away and discard its validity. Even if you have the smallest of inklings, trust it. Even if you have a stirring within your heart but you don't know why, trust it. Even if you feel something but don't quite have proof yet, please trust it.

I've been using the statement lately, "I don't know what's going on, but I know something is going on." That has helped me trust myself even without having evidential proof. I just recognize my feelings, honor myself for having them, and keep going. From there, I just pay attention, making notes of people's behavior, noticing my body responses in certain situations, and collecting my clues. Eventually, the truth will come out, and there will be proof.

If you find that much of this conversation has resonated with you, remember to just acknowledge it, honor the feelings, and hold onto to them. You don't have to *do* anything with them right now. What's really important is that you simply trust and give yourself the space to explore those feelings further.

Now that I've spoken extensively on the Empaths themselves, let's talk about how they receive guidance. Guides will use emotional connection with trinkets, words, signs, and any mundane item to get their attention. When I used to do oracle card readings, sometimes a single word in the whole card description would get my attention. I would feel it reaching out to me as if to say, "I'm the one you need to see." That one word was the message, not necessarily the whole of the statement. At other times, it had nothing to do with the words and everything to do with the picture, color, or even a small item in the card. Point is, I felt the connection to the component rather than taking for granted that the message was about the card itself.

Often when I get messages through clairvoyance or clairaudience, what follows is the emotional response that I am indeed receiving a message. Remember my story of seeing the license plate UR HOME? The reason I knew my Guys were talking to me was because I instantly broke down into tears from feeling the love at the very moment I read the plate. My emotional response was the validation that what I was seeing was meant for me. There wasn't a single doubt that they were comforting me. And in my story of the gypsy trip when I heard, "You know what you need to do. Now do it?" Yeah, instant dread because I knew they were right. I had to face what I was afraid of. I had to throw away my illusion of control and just go. And it was all because I felt they were right. My empath-ness validated what I had heard.

Some of the professions that Empaths might resonate with tend to be careers where they can help other people: crisis counselors, therapists, nurses, hospice caregivers, teachers (of any kind), daycare providers, and art therapists just to name a few. They heal through love and compassion. They give of their hearts. Which is why it is extremely important for the clairsentient to allow themselves to be cared for in return. We need our sanctuary, our trusted companions, and lots of soothing energy when we need to recharge. The most common issue for this group is that they over give. All the time! It's really important to learn to give only when you can and allow yourself to step back when you need to rest. Yes, you will feel guilty. It comes with the territory. But do it anyway! You can't give if you are empty.

CLAIRCOGNIZANT
Clear Knowing – Crown Chakra

This clair category is a curious one indeed. On one side of the room, we've got people that see, hear, and feel things that "aren't there." And on the other side of the room, we have the claircognizants to which the other three are the "airy-fairy" new-agers of the bunch. The claircogs, as I call them, are the facts and figures people. Where logic and reason rule, inspiration comes in the form of sudden moments of brilliance, and any type of guidance that we would call spiritual, they see as their own ingenious nature. These people are our mathematicians, inventors, engineers, scientific discoverers and all that that encompasses.

Don't tell them I told you because they would probably argue with it anyway, but their amazing intelligence comes from the direct connection to Source Energy. They get instant downloads of Divine

Knowledge and Insight through the crown chakra. And the reason they would refute the possibility that it is a spiritual connection is because they simply do not have the external evidence that the other three groups experience. There are no angel whispers, psychic visions, or vibrational barometer readings. It's simply their knowing.

If you are one of these curious creatures, you have probably said, "I don't know how I know. I just know." That's a claircog trait. Ever been working on a project and one final step has you completely stumped? You decide to take a break, go jump in the shower, and within a few minutes, you have a brilliant stroke of genius that completes your project. Yeah, that's a claircog trait, too.

Anytime we over think or push ourselves too hard to find answers, the crown will start to feel stressed and choked. The impatience, judgment, and possible anger that follows will have the chakra shut down. When we do something mundane the crown chakra releases the stress and allows the stream of Divine Knowledge to flow again. By stepping back and taking a break, the crown has a chance to "catch its breath" and relax, bringing the chakra back online. But to tell a claircog that it's because they are connected to Source is a ridiculous claim in their eyes. They just don't see it that way. And that's okay. We don't all have to agree. We don't need to beat our heads against the wall to get them to see it our way. And we don't need to see theirs. Everyone has their place in this world.

Claircogs will almost always gravitate towards careers that are "brain driven." Becoming college professors in their favorite field, seeking a career in physics or quantum mechanics, or going into the space program are some common choices. Some even prefer to be computer programmers and software writers. They are the inventors and scientists that keep our world oh-so-interesting! They crave the nutrient rich information that downloads directly into their brains.

You Can't Convert the Claircogs

I've had couples come to me interested in spiritual coaching, and for some reason, one seems to be an Empath and the other a claircog. The common complaint is that the Empath doesn't feel they can communicate with their logical partner, that they are not on the same page. Typically, they are asking me to work with the claircog to "get them to open up" and "feel" more. Now, what I hear is, "change them so they do it my way." Even if they don't mean it, that is the underlying intention. The Empath is frustrated and out of ideas how to get claircogs to feel their emotions. And I get it. We want to connect with our partners on a deeper level than we do with other people. But anytime we impose our own judgments and attachments on how people should be living, it's never a positive thing.

Once I begin working with the claircog, I actually just help them honor who they are. I offer terminology they resonate with, information to help them assimilate, and validation that they are perfect. No need to change them. There isn't anything wrong with them. They are perfect and in their Divine Expression within this world. Instead, I assist them in understanding their unique style of receiving information while supporting them to get to a place where they can accept themselves wholly. With self-acceptance comes peace and conviction. And then they are better able to help their partner understand who they are and what they need in their relationship. When couples have supportive language around their unique abilities, they are both free to be themselves while being honored for their uniqueness by the other. Isn't that what we're all striving for in our relationships, anyway?

Flip-Flops

My theory is that we are born with all four of these data-collecting systems perfectly intact, giving us the possibility to have all the clairs

123

open and active. It's only when exposed to harsh outside circumstances that we begin to shut them down to protect ourselves. We might live in a family where these kinds of conversations aren't allowed. Or perhaps we experienced a spiritual encounter that frightened us as a child. We learn very quickly as children and young adults to adapt and shift in order to blend in with our families and social environments. If we find ourselves being mistreated or afraid because of these abilities, we'll start to shut them down in order to survive. Remember, a small target is hard to hit.

I also feel we might lean on one more than the others, depending on the life path we've chosen for ourselves before birth. For instance, I feel I was born an Empath because of the kind of work I wanted to do in this lifetime. It affords me a deep connection, compassion, and sense of direction as I navigate through my professional relationships. Clairsentience is my strongest clair, and it's the one I receive information through first.

Yet, I also believe we are capable of healing, opening, and using the ones that might be more dormant. Through the years, I've taught myself how to use the other three by practicing various exercises, letting go of any expectations or fear, and trusting the process. Now, I have a flip-flop kind of thing going where one will validate another and then another. So, I'll *feel* something, *see* a clue validating that feeling, then I'll *know* it's true. Or I'll *hear* a message, *feel* the impact of it in my heart, then I'll *see* the vision in my mind's eye.

Over the years, I've noticed this process happening more quickly, where the different messages are now practically on top of each other. Of course, my curiosity gets me to thinking. If we are born the way we are, with all of these "things" within us, what's stopping us from taking them out and playing with them? Fear probably. Unaware that they are there is a big one. Lack of understanding, sure. All of these reasons are part of the human experience. But it is also up to each one of us to educate ourselves and go beyond the status quo.

> **If you want something you have never had, you must be willing to do something you have never done. –ML**

When it comes right down to it, we are all unique creatures, full of possibility, full of beauty, and full of shit! We're all just trying to do our very best to get through this thing called life. We are working really hard to do that as painlessly as possible. Not one single person has the same path, and no one handles conflict the same as another. We make mistakes, we fall down, and then we get up knowing more than we did before the fall. The bonus part is now, hopefully, you see that you aren't entirely on your own in that endeavor. Not only do you have a Guidance Team eagerly awaiting for you to reach out and connect, but you also have various systems installed allowing you to navigate with clarity and vigor.

We are all different in our abilities. We all have our own unique style of retrieving data, depending on the soul's trajectory in life, our upbringing, our baggage, and what we are open to. Just because someone *can* do it doesn't mean they *allow* themselves do it. Fear is a powerful inhibitor. Don't listen to the fear. It lies. Listen within, listen to your own wisdom. It knows the way.

CHAPTER 7

Honor

I love, love, love talking about boundaries! They are so important to have, and yet, it seems to be such a taboo conversation for people. You know, the ones that are whispered about in dark corners at dinner parties. We scurry and hide from the judgment that comes our way when we try to draw our line in the sand. The reactions of horror from people that we would have the gall to not allow their hatred, harm, and abuse. It's time to rip open the curtains and shed some much needed light on this topic. No more shall we feel shame for wanting to take care of ourselves. No more will we apologize for putting ourselves first and honoring the energy being that we are. Today, we begin a new conversation.

It's All About the Love

I'm not going to fluff this up for you, cultivating healthy boundaries is a tricky bitch! Wanting them is considered selfish, enforcing them is a balancing act, and maintaining them is a 24/7 job. Remember in the last chapter when we talked about the cellular membrane and how you had zero control with what happens on the outside of that bubble? Well, this is the follow-up conversation. And where that is most definitely true, the power you have, and where you apply it makes all the difference in the world. By no means am I saying that we have to take the abuse just because we have no control over their actions. Au contraire! All the power resides in our responsiveness and willingness to be in action for our overall well-being.

The only reason we even need boundaries is because everyone has their own preferences of how they would like to be treated, as well as each having their own style in which they treat others. We all have our own battle scars and baggage that shape how we relate to other humans. Time and time again, we allow people to stomp all over our hearts without even a whisper of a no. We justify it and excuse it away, typically blaming ourselves and thinking we probably deserved it on some level. We say yes, when we really meant no, leaving that wretched feeling of remorse, shame, and self-loathing because we swallowed our voice when we knew better. It truly is a sea of crashing waves to navigate through. And let's face it, most of us aren't that great at sailing.

And why do we allow it? Why do we let our boundaries wither away to nothing? Why do we let people get away with taking too much of our time, energy, love, and vitality? Well, for love of course. We all want it, and we're willing to do just about anything to get it. Sometimes, even harming ourselves in the process. Regardless of the lifestyle we live, our belief system, where we were born, or what kind of hobbies we enjoy, it is the driving force for all of our choices in relationships. We want so badly to be accepted by our peers, by our families, and by people we may never actually meet. We let others say and do things that go against what we know to be right for us in the hopes they will like us. Little by little…bit by bit…we sell out for love. If we don't rock the boat too much, if we give in and say yes, if we just let them have their way because it's what they want, all will be well. Like a marble statue, we are slowly chiseled down into an unrecognizable version of who we really are. We allow our identities to be reshaped into a form that makes others happy, dwindling ourselves down to make them comfortable with who we are. All for the love and acceptance we hope is at the end of the ordeal.

Empty Calories

This kind of human behavior isn't formed overnight. It starts at a very early age when all we want is daddy's praise and mommy's love. Many of us come from neglected, even sometimes abusive situations in our childhoods. This ignites within us the drive to seek love through other avenues. We grow up and go searching for surrogate-type parental units to give us what our real parents didn't. Everyone, on some level, is seeking someone to help heal the inner child wounds that are buried deep down inside.

And remember, we're all different; so again, this isn't going to be a cookie-cutter conversation. No one formula exists that fits everyone. We all have different versions of the story but the energy is always the same. If, for instance, you didn't have a nurturing relationship with your father, as an adult you might date men that have some of the same personality traits or mannerisms that he possessed (whether you're aware of it or not). Or, if you were raised with a domineering, verbally abusive father figure, you might seek out strong males to "take care of you." On the surface, it feels somewhat safe because you are familiar with this behavior. But what's going on under the surface is that you are seeking the love from that particular archetype to stave off the feelings of neglect you experienced from your father.

We're all trying to make it up to ourselves while simultaneously trying to prove to our caretakers that we are, in fact lovable, that we do have worth. Sadly, these types of adult relationships rarely nurture and support us on a real level. They have no nutritional value much like the empty calories of a candy bar.

> **If we aren't watchful of our desperation to *just* be loved, we might let *just* anybody love us. –ML**

If our predominant motivation is to be accepted, but we've been told over and over again that we are unwanted, we will work feverishly to find someone to validate our worth. Something deep within is trying to show the world that we matter, frantically running around the globe, grabbing onto anyone that might prove it. Prove to us, to them, and to the one who hurt us. It's a vicious, unending cycle of emptiness.

That emptiness is the very reason we perpetuate the pattern of abuse and rejection. Anytime we chase after relationships in desperation, those choices probably won't be good ones. We'll keep glomming onto anyone in the hopes they are going to heal us. The pattern continues because we keep picking people that "look" like the parental figure. We will never fill the holes of our wounds with other relationships. No matter how many people we meet, marry, date, like, love, or befriend. If we constantly scramble around trying to find someone to love us just to prove we are lovable, that hole will never get filled. No one will ever love us enough to heal the wounds inflicted by the neglecting parent.

Truly, to heal this wound we must love and accept ourselves the way we are wanting others to. That is the magickal formula of being free from these patterns. And I know it's been said to death, but if we don't first love ourselves, how can we allow anyone to truly love us. If we choose to drag around the old stories and continue to allow the negating patterns, we'll never feel worthy of the love we are being offered by others. We will subconsciously push it away and only accept the level we have grown accustomed to. That is all we can allow because it is all that we trust. But, the moment we decide to believe a new story, one that supports the beautiful being we are, everything changes. Eventually, our patterns will begin to shift and our awareness will expand. The power of these programs that linger over us will diminish, leading us to relationships with nutritional value.

Breaking Down the Walls

Anytime we carry within us a belief that we don't matter in the world, there will be ZERO boundaries. I mean, why bother? If we don't have anything of value to offer, why protect ourselves, right? Boundaries won't be needed. But man, the world can be rough. We learn very quickly how to build up walls in order to have some sort of protection from life's beatings. Closing off, shutting down the heart, and hardening ourselves seems to be the only way to get through our days. Our skewed perception makes us believe this is the only way we are going to survive. So, we build.

The only problem with that plan is that when we close down, we also cut off the flow from Source and shut down our Emotional Guidance System (our link to our Divine Wisdom). We harden and become rigid in our physical bodies. We live in fear and stay ready to run at the first sign of danger. We miss out on amazing new adventures that could change the course of our lives. We'll shy away from offers to climb mountains and swim in the seas. Little by little, our trust diminishes, and our faith wanes.

We create walls, tall, impenetrable brick walls. Walls that close us off from the rest of the world. Thick bricks that, yes, may keep us safe, but they also hold us prisoner. This only perpetuates a deeper lack of motivation, passion, and low self-worth, taking us further into isolation. It's like cutting off your arm if you are a master painter. There is no point to life when you have cut off the very reason you were born. And we were born to love and to be loved. Our purpose is to connect with each other on very real levels. To show our hearts, and to be shown another's in return. So sure, you may be the princess in the tower, safe and high enough to see all the land, but you are alone.

Boundaries

Being a prisoner of our own making is not the life we were born for. Souls come here to connect on a physical and emotional level, to experience each other in relatable ways. When we're able to exchange our thoughts, ideas, and experiences with others, we become inspired. We take risks when we are filled with passion and joy. When we stay open to possibilities, we try new flavors, expanding our awareness of the world in which we live. So then what do we do? If the human experience can feel like one big war zone but we were created to be open and connected, how do we have the openness but not the pain?

Boundaries baby! If walls are the frequency of fear, then boundaries are the frequency of love. If I were to have walls around me, I'm basically saying, "I'm afraid of what you might do to me so rather than risk it, I'm not going to give you access." This cuts off any chance of having new and exciting possibilities. What if that person wanted to invite you to Paris because their travel buddy got sick at the last minute? You won't know this because there was never a chance for them to ask you. You missed out on something awesome just because your norm was to be closed off from the world.

But when one has boundaries, in essence they are saying, "I love myself enough to not let you harm me." It is the act of loving yourself enough to say no when you would typically allow it. To walk away when someone has crossed the line is one of the bravest things you can do for yourself. To end relationships when they have become toxic is a powerful declaration that you deserve better. Choosing to honor the being that you are, loving yourself above all others, and taking care of your own heart is a true revolutionary act. This is what it means to have healthy boundaries.

Yes, many will say that is a selfish act. And I agree! Wholeheartedly agree! If anything, we should be selfish when it comes to our personal safety and well-being. We should be selfish when we are watching over our own hearts. We must be selfish with our time and where we spend it, making sure that it is valued by those we are giving it to. Selfishness is the ability to care for self. It's no one else's job. Doesn't it make sense to be selfish if what we're talking about is valuing yourself enough to allow love in your life?

Side Note: For clarification, I don't mean to say that there isn't a shadow side to the word selfish. There is. If you believe you are more important than others and it doesn't matter who you hurt in your quest to take care of Numero Uno, that is your shadow. If you are harming others by putting yourself first, you may need to look at that and have some accountability. What I'm talking about is caring for self, but not at the cost of another. Sadly, many of us tend to care for others at the cost of ourselves. And that's just bad math!

You Have Three Options

Imagine if you will, that you are the princess (or prince) standing in the center of court, looking around, taking in the view. As you navigate the conversation of walls versus boundaries, ponder these options and decide which would best support you as a whole.

Option #1: There are no castle walls. Your kingdom is exposed and open to being attacked and overthrown at any time. No one is watching for enemies in the distance and even if you saw them coming, there wouldn't be a way to stop them. There is no safety, and you feel vulnerable and exposed for what might happen at any moment. This causes fear and stress to be the dominant experience.

Option #2: Behind you, to your left and to your right, are castle walls. In front of you is the drawbridge and iron gates, closed and securely sealed, locking everyone out. And everyone in. No one can leave, and no one can enter, including the neighboring merchants with fresh food, supplies, and provisions. You may be safe but you're isolated as well. And even though you look around at the starving people of your Kingdom, you do not open the gates. Hope is lost.

Option #3: The castle gates are wide open but there are guards at the gates, monitoring who comes in and what business they have for your Kingdom. They decide who comes and who goes, keeping everyone safe in their diligence and fortitude. Never once letting their gaze wander from the task at hand. All visitors are inquired about, merchants and thieves alike. No one passes without just cause and virtuous intention. The people thrive and the Kingdom is safe.

Real Life Translation

It's apparent that in these modern times not many of us have lived in an actual castle, but we can probably appreciate the visual. I would bet that at some point we have all experienced living within metaphorical castle walls. Experiencing even the slightest bit of a broken heart is enough to close the castle gates, fill up the moat, and ready the archers.

In our first option, our hearts are wide open, allowing anyone to just walk in with their muddy boots and stomp all over us. They can say or do anything without us muttering a single peep in defense for ourselves. This is typically how we are born, open and exposed. But inevitably, something hurts us and we learn very quickly that it doesn't work being that open. So to protect our fragile hearts, we react in a knee-jerk type response and slam the doors shut. This takes us to the second option.

We close down, harden our hearts, and toughen up. All for the sake of survival. But in the end, we cut off our supply from others that might love us back as well as the Divine love from Source. Our body loses vitality and drive, our heart misses connection, and eventually apathy sets in. Some might think this is what boundaries look like and in a world full of pain it's the only way to get through it. But they are mistaken. True boundaries never cut you off from your supply. They only enhance that connection.

Personally, the third option is the only option for me! Neither exposed and stomped on, nor shut down and numb, in this space we find a true balance. I'm talking about wide open but being completely in charge of who and what comes in. Being so very clear where your line is drawn in the sand, you watch your people and remind them where it is if they forget. Having such an intensely aware relationship with your own heart so that you know exactly what you need to feel loved and supported is a powerful compass along the journey of life. Now that is living the life of a powerful being indeed.

Making a List, Checking it Twice

Okay, so we need boundaries. You might be thinking "great, now what?" Well, this is where the journey gets very personal. You are your own person, after all. You have needs, quirks, desires, and wounds. The boundaries you require and cultivate will be your own.

But, before you can enact boundaries you must first be aware of what they look like. The first step is to get clear with your own personal likes and dislikes in relation to other people. And I don't necessarily mean outside of you. Let's take the conversation inward and strengthen your awareness of how you feel in these moments. How do you like being treated? When someone shows you kindness and respect, what does that feel like in your body? When you are scolded, attacked, or shamed, how does your physical body react? Do you feel pain? Is it sharp or dull? Is there stress in the muscles? Or is it more within your organ systems? Is it localized? Or maybe an overall sense of heaviness? And each time it happens do you feel it in the same way and/or same area? Get as detailed and focused as you can with whatever you are experiencing in that moment.

I'm a huge fan of combining the sensations of the physical body with honoring the wisdom of our emotions. Those two checkpoints are critical when cultivating self-awareness and can tell you so much about your relationships. If you do not know how you feel, how can you know if something supports you? Noting how certain events "hit you" will help you determine whether or not you want to participate in them. Your feelings strengthen your awareness in the moment, helping you figure that out sooner rather than days, weeks, or even years later.

When we've come from neglectful, abusive situations we have mastered a sort of stylized-reactive-survival-coping-mechanism-thing. Part of that mechanism is the ability to become numb to what is happening to us. It allows us to stay in denial and removed from the awareness that we need to take action for our own well-being. Therefore, we aren't present when our boundaries are being crossed because we are reverting back to our old ways of escapism and survival. In order for us to reprogram these old responses, we must get into a conversation that creates new pathways in our thinking. When all else fails, try a new tactic!

Start practicing what it feels like to be present in your conversations. All conversations. Invite your Sacred Observer to watch over what is happening in that moment. Be present enough with the person you are talking to, but also pay attention to the whole picture. When people are talking to you what sensations are happening in you? Is it a good feeling or not-so-good feeling? Does it "hit you" in that same spot each time you talk to a specific person? Is it the person or that particular topic that feels off? When you walk away, are you enlivened or drained? Does it happen every time you're with that same person? Or perhaps each time you visit that particular location? Any and all questions are valid and can be a strong tool in navigating your day-to-day experience. Asking the right questions leads to the right answers.

Practice The Art of Awareness!

The more…

→self-awareness is cultivated

    →you choose what feels good

        →you'll walk away from what doesn't

            →you will make yourself a priority

                →you'll create healthy boundaries

See how that works?

Inspired Assignment: Grab two sheets of paper. On the top of one write "What I Will Allow." On the other write "What I Won't Allow." Start by writing things down on the appropriate list that you already know. Try to be as detailed as you can without writing out actual experiences you've had. Example: instead of writing "I didn't like it when Becky told me to shut up yesterday," say something like "I don't like being told to shut up." By making it a full spectrum statement rather than that one instance, you are setting up a program to have boundaries when anyone says this to you, not just Becky.

Once you have a good chunk of items listed, hang the papers up where you will see them but in a place where you have privacy. (It isn't helpful if we have people around that mock us for trying exercises like this.) As you move in and out of your day, make note of new awarenesses of likes and dislikes and add them to your lists.

Little by little, you are training your brain to see boundary infractions and to quickly determine if you are okay with it or not. This cuts down your reaction and response time so the infraction gets handled as quickly as possible. You are literally retraining your brain to function in a way that supports you rather than going numb and allowing people to treat you any old way. It sounds like a remedial kind of exercise, but trust me, it's going to make sense the further you go. With patience and practice, you'll eventually be in the moment and will be able to hold your line without going numb.

The Key: Please don't beat yourself up in this process. Adding judgment and criticism to any personal growth exercise will only prolong your progress. Be gentle with yourself throughout this journey. Give your inner critic's voice a vacation and keep playing!

Training Your People

When I joined the workforce, my first few jobs centered around restaurant and bar service. Understandably, with each new job there would follow new policies and procedures to learn. So the training began. The MOD (manager on duty) would walk me through various levels of the business to properly prepare me to at least meet, but hopefully exceed their expectations. If I did well, I was rewarded with an approving nod. If I failed, they would pull me aside and ask me to correct the behavior. Being a natural born people pleaser, I aimed for the nods which made me a good employee over the years. Little did I know then that this structured, albeit mundane teaching process, would play such a large role in the healthy boundaries conversations of my future coaching business. Looking back, I can now see how it was the perfect parable for this topic.

When clients come to see me in search of stronger boundaries my response is always, you have to train your people. Which is instantly followed by an odd look and rejecting body language. See, for people pleasers, that statement is quite the trigger. To consider participating in their own experience, molding and crafting it to be proactive rather than just letting people run amok, is a hard concept to immediately land on. And the statement itself evokes a sense of controlling or manipulating people, but it isn't at all what I mean.

People treat you the way they do because it's been agreed upon over the weeks, months, and years of the relationship. Each of you came to the table announcing who and what you would be for the other. Both parties agreed, shook hands, and started acting in that manner. And maybe at the time you thought it was a pretty sweet deal, but eventually started realizing you don't like the agreement at all. Only you don't know exactly how to say you don't want to play anymore, so you stay quiet in order to keep the peace.

By being non-resistant and passive, you have subliminally given them permission to treat you however they choose. Whether you like their treatment or not. And for them, there isn't an issue because they feel they have your permission. How are they to know you don't like being treated like that if you've never made them aware of your feelings about it? They are simply playing by the rules of the game you have both agreed upon. If at some point you realize you don't like the game anymore, it is well within your right to change the rules. It is up to you to speak up, to inform them of how you want to be treated going forward. They will never know if you don't explain. And so their training begins.

Let's do another flow chart thingy to explain how to have these difficult conversations. As always, it is a jumping off point. Redesign it to fit your own needs and circumstance.

Someone says or does something to you that feels uncomfortable and unwanted...

- First ask yourself, "Am I okay with this?" I know it sounds silly, but so many times we don't even register when something hurts us. If the answer is yes, then let it go and move on. If the answer is no...

- Go within to get really clear about how you feel. There's no need to rush. Spend some time formulating the words to be able to express to yourself how it makes you feel. This step is more for you than it is for them. You must have the clarity of your own feelings before you are able to express them to others. Once you know how it made you feel...

- Prepare. Create a 1-2 sentence statement that perfectly expresses what they did and how it makes you feel. Remember, to keep it about you, not about attacking or judging them. You are simply saying to them, that thing you did doesn't feel good to me. Spend as much time as you need with this. Again, there's no need to rush the process. Once you're ready...

- Now you speak it to them. You are inviting them to stop that behavior. It might sound a little like this:
  - When you...belittled me, teased me, cut me off...
  - I feel/felt...sad, hurt, ashamed, embarrassed...
  - And it made me think that you...don't love me, don't respect me...

- Next step, stop talking. Let them respond, watch their reaction. They'll either get defensive and justify their actions, hurting you more or apologize and agree to not do that again.

Remember to speak from a place of love and honesty. Tell them you understand this is the way it's always been but that you are asking for it to be another way. Give them an example perhaps of how you would like it moving forward. Offer it. Invite them. If you demand or attack, the outcome will not be favorable. People that love you are willing to treat you the way you want. And when you simply come from a space of invitation, they are more likely to accept.

Going forward, it is your responsibility to help them remember the new agreement if they forget. Sometimes, habits are hard to break and they'll slip up from time to time, reverting to the old way. That's okay. Just lovingly remind them. Again, when people love you they are willing to work with you. They won't mind the reminders.

You Are the Writer of Your Rules

You are the center of your own universe. This life that you are living, is well, yours. The world does in fact, revolve around you. Relatively speaking, that is. Wouldn't it be safe to say that you have the right to oversee what you will allow and won't allow? That beautiful bubble of yours is brimming with magick. Everything in it, your words, thoughts, feelings, choices…all yours! So you get to write the rules. You are in charge of educating people about how you would like to be treated. You are the writer of the script in the play called "This is My Amazing Life!" You have say over how it goes. And if you didn't know that until now, well, welcome to the party!

The power of your free will states that you can choose ANYTHING. If you like something, go towards it and have more. If you aren't a fan of what just went down, you have the right to move away from it. No one can do that for you and nor do they have the power to make you do anything you don't want to. That is of course, unless you give them that power.

The overall goal is to enforce the rules of the game by drawing a clear line and asking your people to honor it. All without harming the other players. We're not aiming to be a belligerent jerk, aggressively bending their will. Hurting someone just because they've hurt you never brings you peace. Revenge is a shadow attribute and could never bring you into alignment with yourself. It's a reactive response that stems from a place of hurt and anger. To me, that's never the point to doing this kind of work.

What we're truly going for is a simple invitation to renegotiate the relationship. You have grown and are now aware that the behaviors no longer work for you. So, you are presenting possible upgrades and amendments to the previously agreed upon relationship. It's an invitation because they do not have to comply. They can disagree and walk away. You are not trying to control or manipulate. (Which by the way, not speaking up when they've harmed you just to keep them in your life is still a form of manipulation.) You are asking them to consider these changes because you see the relationship is worth it.

That's not to say they will always be happy when you've presented these amendments. Not everyone likes being asked to change their behavior, especially if they are benefiting from the way the game is currently set up. Some people enjoy the exchange of energy from passive people and prefer having the upper hand. But remember, this isn't a negotiation on whether or not you are allowed boundaries. It's negotiating whether or not the relationship will continue to move forward based on their response.

The first important step is to become clear with your lists. Knowing what you will and won't allow in life is crucial. Knowing where your line is drawn in the sand makes it so much easier to maintain your boundaries with people. Without that clarity, the line gets fuzzy and can be easily moved, stepped on, or washed away without your say so.

Like a Hawk

I have a saying that I live by:

> **"Alive or dead, human or non-human, friend or foe –
> everyone gets the same boundaries."**

This mantra is my little reminder to hold my line, to be equally fair to all players of the game in my life. If I give one person lax boundaries but maintain a hard line for another, it will get confusing. Not only for them but for myself as well. They won't know how to treat me if they don't see a consistency. And I'll have a hard time keeping up with what I told each person if I'm being wishy-washy. Really, it's about ease. By keeping the same line for all relationships, I have an easier time remembering my lists. And by staying consistent, my people have an easier time remembering the new rules. If they don't know from one minute to the next what my boundaries are, they will end up reverting to their old routine and treat me the way they've always done. We are creatures of habit, after all.

On another note, you might have noticed the "alive or dead, human or non-human" part of that statement. It's odd I know, but let me explain. In my line of work, I sometimes come into contact with not-just-living-humans. And not all of them are "good guys." Some of them can get downright nasty! I conduct myself the same across the board, regardless. Whether I'm giving a reading, conducting a paranormal investigation, or hanging out with friends at brunch, my line is clearly marked for all to see. I wouldn't let a stranger mistreat me, so why would I let my best friend? If I'm trying to sleep, I wouldn't let just anyone come to my house at 3:00 a.m. and bang on my door for no good reason, right? Then, why would I let a deceased human spirit wake me up just to talk? Same goes for non-human beings. I'm not going to allow a darker entity to push me around if I wouldn't let me someone I love do it.

The bottom line is I watch *everyone*. Those who love me and those that hate me and everyone in between. I hold the line regardless of who is standing at it. The truth is boundaries are never about the other person, anyway. It doesn't have anything to do with anyone else but ourselves. The boundaries I put in place are more to monitor myself than anything. I'm the one that has allowed harmful, toxic people to abuse me. I have let them walk in without question and take anything they wanted. I seem to have this little thing about me that gets me into trouble. I trust. Blindly. And If I'm not mindful, I'll trust those that intend to do harm. It isn't that I believe everyone is out to get me, just in case it's starting to sound like that. I need the systems, visual aids, and checkpoints to remind myself to be the guards at the gate.

In our race to be loved and accepted, we have forgotten ourselves. Over time, we have diminished what we stand for. We have created this weird negotiation-type conversation to make us seem like we are creating boundaries when really we're just asking for permission. We ask the other person if they are okay with our line. We back down at any little push because we're afraid they might reject us and leave. It perpetuates the constant need for validation and eventually, the selling out for love.

My boundaries aren't negotiable. They are drawn. Clear as day. And when someone steps over the line, I lovingly remind them that I'm not okay with that. If it happens again, I might be a little bit more insistent that they respect that line. But by the third or fourth time, I'm done. If that person isn't showing signs of respect and they aren't attempting to remember and work with me, then why would I keep letting them in my space? They've already made it clear they don't care about my well-being. Why would I keep investing in that relationship if it's obvious they aren't willing to invest in me?

Let's Be Fair

I think it's pretty fair to say it isn't their fault if they don't know what your boundaries are. You can't take it for granted that they know. So, your first task (after you're clear about what you need) is to speak those boundaries out loud. Tell them! Give them a heads-up that you are changing the rules of your life. You can't be upset with them if they don't know. So, be sure to play fair!

A lot of human conflicts seem to stem from people assuming that others know what we want. But they don't. For me, that conversation typically sounds something like this: "I'm not sure if you knew this or not, but I'm trying this new thing where I honor myself and speak up when I feel like my boundaries have been crossed. I just wanted to let you know, that thing you did (explain what happened, just the facts) made me feel (describe the emotion) and I thought (whatever it made you think how they felt about you). Can I ask for (insert new rule) instead? Would you be willing to work with me on that?"

The first note I want to point out is anytime you go to someone with this conversation, you want to go to them in a non-attack mode. Be honest, but inviting. You are essentially saying, "I love our relationship, and I'm willing to work on it. Are you?" If you go to them and accuse them of being a bad friend and projecting your judgments and speculations with anger, you are asking for an argument, and it will not end well. Most people fear confrontations, thinking that if they say anything at all, it will incite an argument. But there is always a way to speak your truth without harm.

I highly recommend taking your time with your words. Get very clear with what happened, how it felt, where it lands in your body, and what doesn't work for you. Ground, center, and meditate a little if that helps. Prepare your words, and check to make sure it's really what you want to say. Don't water it down because you think they won't be able to handle it. Believe in your own truth. Double check your motives, and make sure you're coming from a place of loving them and loving yourself. Then, go talk to them, and be as clear as you can.

Inspired Assignment: Speak your truth without harm. Easier said than done, right? But it is possible.

The Goal: To be so present to how you feel about a situation and then to formulate words to express those feelings, all the while delivering them without causing any harm. That, my dear, is mastery. Even if the conversation gets loud and heated, you can still remain centered and present.

A few tricks of the trade:

•Stay calm. Keep your voice soft but confident – not weak and passive, nor aggressive

•Don't get caught up in who's right and who's wrong - that's not the point

•Don't project your judgments and criticisms onto them

•Don't blame or "one up" the other person. It's not a contest

•Be open to hearing their perspective

•Be open to being wrong – you might learn something about yourself

•Remember the goal: to be heard while simultaneously strengthening your relationship moving forward

It takes practice, so don't stress about getting it right the first time. You will fumble your words, revert to old habits, and stick your foot in your mouth more than once. But keep working on it. Be open to walking away with more clarity for not only who they are in your life but also who you are. We can always learn something in these moments. Before long, the truth will come out, and you'll be able to deliver it with love and respect.

My Guys say, "This is why it's called Language Arts. Because it is an art form to speak the truth without harm."

Shut Up and Listen!

You've done so much work to get to this point. You have practiced staying aware in times when you would normally shrink away and stay numb. You are gaining more and more clarity for what you want in your relationships. And you are building your powerful vocabulary to be able to communicate the truth without hurting those you care about. All of this hard work has been focused inward. It was all about you connecting to your authentic voice. This was about bringing yourself to a state of full awareness at all times. It was also to show you how your choices make all the difference in the world as to whether or not you are enjoying the ride. So, now we take all the practice, knowledge, and skills you've acquired, and we go outward. Into the world! This is what we've been training for!

Something very interesting happens when you start changing the rules of your own game. When you've gotten clear about where your line is, and you are consistent with standing your ground, people start showing you their true colors. That is both the good news and equally, the bad news. Good news because you now know what their true agendas are. And bad news, if that means they don't really care about you the way you thought they did. But knowing is always better than not knowing, I think. It can be eye-opening to see a person's true motive.

Let's say you have had an experience that you are not okay with. From within, you have collected your thoughts and formed your words. Then you succinctly speak those words out loud with love and compassion, but with a dash of conviction. The very next thing you're going to want to do is SHUT UP! Stop talking and wait. Let them respond. But pay very close attention to that response. Listen to their words and tone, and watch their body language. Closely. Intently. And why is that so important, you might ask? Because the very first thing that comes out of their mouths will tell you who they are in your life. This first sentence will tell you whether or not they are someone you want to continue to walk with or move away from. Yeah, it's pretty important.

I've noticed over the years, as I practice my own boundaries, that people generally respond two different ways. People who love you are going to naturally want to support you. Their agenda is usually one of love and nurturing, so they may be unaware that they've done something to cause you upset. When you come to them and ask them if they are willing to work on that behavior, their immediate response will be of shock and remorse, followed by apology and agreement. They will genuinely feel bad because they hurt you. People who love you typically don't want to do things that cause harm. It's pretty easy math.

But if they respond in any way, shape, or form that sounds like they are degrading or belittling you, playing it off like it's no big deal, or shaming you for having those feelings...well, let's just say they aren't there to love you. These are typically the people who are benefitting from your lack of boundaries. They are the ones hoping you don't catch on to all the soul-sucking they've been doing (whether they're aware of it or not). They are not for you, my dear. Their agenda is to get something from you. This is the bad news I talked about before. Once you see it, you can't unsee it. And I'll be honest, it breaks my heart every single time I see this in someone I love. But the issue is they don't care about me in the same way. Their "love" is generally toxic, manipulative, and controlling. They are greatly benefiting from what I give them, but not giving me the same.

When you see this type of response, it is extremely important to stop sharing your heart with them immediately, and find your exit strategy. Stop telling them your dreams. Stop giving them your energy. And start formulating a plan to remove yourself as soon as possible, because they are more than likely sucking the life out of you and are hoping you never figure it out.

I know this is a hard conversation to have and an even more difficult step to take. I've been there. It feels extremely counter-intuitive, especially being an Empath. I kept thinking that if I love them enough, they'll change. If I could just give them more, they'll see that I really love them, and they'll give it back to me. No! They don't. They won't. And at some point, I had to understand, *really* understand that it wasn't my job to heal them. I had to accept that some people just don't know how to be loved the right way, and no amount of love you show them will change that.

Now of course, there is a middle of the road to this tale. There are people leeching off of you but they are not aware that they are harming you. Perhaps life has been a difficult journey, leaving them a little weathered and worn. They see you as a shining light in their darkness and have glommed onto you for safety and security. You don't necessarily have to break up with these people but you do want to move them away from you just a bit. Give them the space to make it on their own and space for you to be able to breathe. You are not meant to be their savior.

Now here's the bonus question. A big step when doing your own shadow work is asking yourself why do you believe that it is your job to save them? What is in you that is addicted to being the rescuer? Because it isn't appropriate to be carrying them around like that. We are all responsible for our own growth. No one person is meant to carry the whole. If you can, question the program within you that believes it's your responsibility and give it permission to let go and let them do it.

Opening that conversation within you leads to the possibility of healing the wound and releasing the story around it. Thus, freeing you from its powerful influence. It untethers the stories that your value is wrapped up in their wellness and allows you to re-write a story of your choosing. Simultaneously, it offers them the chance to see the strength within themselves to stand up on their own and flourish in life. Lovingly support them to "get it" themselves, but love them through it. It's up to you to decide how much that will be. There is a perfect place for you both, where you are both loved and supported by each other and can feel enlivened, not drained.

Remember, not everyone will agree with your boundaries. Some will outright be angry that you have the nerve to enforce such things. (These are the ones you're going to want to keep an eye out for.) But, it isn't up for negotiation. These are the things you are stating you need to feel loved, honored, and respected. If someone loves you, that is exactly what they will want to give you. When you enforce your boundaries, some people will fall away. They will make you the bad guy and will leave you. Good. Let them. That opens up space for new people who will instantly love who you are and honor the boundaries you have laid out. And that's the best news of all!

Walking along your path of life, you've been who you've been. People have come to know you in the manner you have presented. They go into relationship agreements based on the version you have broadcasted into the world. You are this, and they are that. Perfect fit. Or so you think. Maybe it is. Maybe it isn't. Perhaps being this version was good for that moment, but down the line you grew out of that and into a new you. Throughout this conversation you might be realizing your boundaries need a little work. Or perhaps they are almost non-existent, and you want to be more proactive in that area of your life.

Immediately, you shift from unaware to aware. The two lists come closer into view, and you begin to formulate where that line is and how you will choose to enforce it.

Each time you take a stand for your boundaries, the more you are cultivating self-trust. You are claiming that you have value in this world. You are taking a powerful stand to receive good things in life. For each toxic person you move out of your space, a new healthy and loving person can step in. You do deserve the love you give others. Start by giving that love to yourself first. Others will soon follow.

I promise!

CHAPTER 8

Harmony

There are two halves (and a million facets) to every human. The physical humanness is but a mere 50% of the equation. But it's such a fun part, wouldn't you agree? It's the beautiful vehicle in which we get to do things like drive, dance, run, have sex, scream, eat ice cream, and poop. In this state-of-the-art meat suit we have a lovely little thing called the ego which allows us the fullest extent of our human experience.

The other half of this magnificent existence is the higher awareness, the soul side of the equation. This is the essence that knows we exist beyond our meat suit. It's the awareness of "something more" in an otherwise limited reality. On the human side, everything is really *real* and very dangerous. But our soul knows we are a part of the whole cosmic order, and with that comes a peace within our existence.

Gnothi Seauton - Know Thyself

Did you know that the only reason for our existence was simply to know ourselves? That's it. That's the BIG mystery that everyone is running around trying to figure out. Oh, I don't mean who you are as a human. I mean the whole picture. The whole enchilada of existence. We come to Earth to have experiences so that the soul knows more about itself when it returns whence it came. The macrocosm awareness of being a soul can only be known as such by choosing to be incarnated as a puny human. As a spirit, floating up in "wherever we come from," we can only have the consciousness that we are Divine by coming to

Earth and having the full corporeal experience. Without that contrast, we simply will not know ourselves. It's through interaction, relation, and opposition that we experience consciousness of self. That's one tasty enchilada!

Then once we do crash land into our human bodies, we double down our bets and jump into the rat race. Every second of every day we are judging, accepting, and rejecting something or someone within our field of vision. Every instance we do this the data gets filed away within our psyche (and ultimately our soul's awareness) to strengthen the construct of the identity of self.

Look at it another way. Imagine there is a red dot painted on someone's wall. But there wasn't anything else to see, know, experience, or witness to contrast against. How would she know she was a red dot? Did someone tell her? Who? Maybe that blue dot over there? In order for the red dot to know herself, she must have the contrasting experience of the blue dot. In that flash of a moment, identity is born because the blue dot has validated the red dot's existence in his witnessing of her. It's in that witnessing (being seen, heard, touched, experienced, etc.) that the red dot knows of her own existence. Without it, there would be no awareness of self.

Now, that's not to say it must always be the opposite experience. We also birth awareness by seeing ourselves in another. If the red dot saw another red dot, they would have connection rather than a stark contrast. And in connection they would create a relationship. They are capable of relating to one another because they see themselves in each other. But the two dots know they are individual, each maintaining their own identity. They would both have a deeper sense of awareness because they are the same color, but not the same dot. Here is where humanity begins to create a tribal mentality, coming together in our likeness and supporting each other in our shared interests.

In essence, we come to Earth, being our individual self, looking out in the world and seeing, hearing, feeling, experiencing, loving, hating, wanting, and rejecting all that life has to offer. Through every choice of either drawing it closer to us or pushing it away, we are getting to know ourselves. Whether we draw something in to have connection with it or we reject what is being offered, we are constructing a stronger sense of identity with each choice.

I like cheeseburgers but I don't like bell peppers. I prefer ladybugs to crawl on me but not spiders. When I'm sad, I want to listen to coffee house-type music, and when I'm PMS-ing, I love listening to rock. It's in the awareness of my likes and dislikes that I know myself on a deeper level. I love open-minded discussions about quantum physics, but I don't want to contribute to conversations that are gossip. I'm an advocate for human rights for all and detest manipulative, abusive tactics to control others. I know myself more because of these contrasts. And the more I know myself, the more I know who I want in my circle. I choose my relationships based on who I know myself to be. This duality births my beliefs and passions, and in turn, will dictate the course I steer through life. How can I choose my direction without the awareness for these things?

I know these personality traits and preferences seem pretty simple and even obvious when we discuss human life. But "in the back of house," in our psyche and subconscious, it plays a very large role in the choices we'll make. It influences whether or not we'll have strong boundaries and what we will stand up and fight for. If we don't explore these questions, we have the tendency to lose ourselves in the mix of trying to make everyone okay with us. We sell out over and over again for the love and acceptance of others. We'll squelch our inner truth for the safety of blending in. And our decision-making process will be externally driven in the hopes that everyone will like us. So many issues come from that place of not knowing ourselves. Our passions, platforms, and soapboxes get muddied up and we buckle at the slightest bit of pressure to conform.

Side Note: As a Medium, I feel this formula of identity relates to the deceased as well. Through the years of being a paranormal investigator, I would find earthbound spirits who had actually forgotten that they had died. It's as if they have some sort of amnesia to the fact that they no longer had a corporeal existence. And think about it, if no one ever talked to you again, looked at you, touched you, or interacted with you…wouldn't you start questioning your own existence as well? I think I would.

My theory is these are the spirits we would call classic hauntings. If they worked in a hospital while they were alive, they would have spent their days taking care of the sick, overseeing the care of the patients, and being responsible for the cleanliness of their area. In death, they would feel compelled to do these same tasks. If they worked as a chambermaid in a hotel, you guessed it, they would be making beds and laying out fresh linens even in death.

During the investigations, I started to notice the longer they had been dead, the stronger the amnesia. For instance, a person that lived in the 1800's would be more embedded in their own "reality" than someone who passed 30 years ago. A consistent and important factor was that these souls hadn't yet "crossed over," which is the very definition of an earthbound spirit. This means they are still connected to their personality, emotions, and mental state as when they were alive. Crossing over is the act of passing through the veil and returning to our spiritual status. When a soul crosses over, they shed their personality traits and remember their Divineness.

So, as the years pass and human contact ceases, the earthbound's self-awareness would diminish, leaving them to question their own existence. And since there are few things more frightening for a human than losing their identity, to comfort themselves they would go to a place that felt familiar, a place they knew they belonged and could do the things they remembered doing. This would provide them a glimpse into their past, validating their existence. Of course, this is purely my own theory, but it was the case in every ghostly encounter. So, I'm sticking with it.

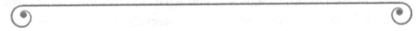

Light Ego

Like a surgeon, we are going to gently open up this massive conversation of what it means to exist. We'll deconstruct the different components, peel back and look at each beautiful layer that makes up the spiritual human. First, we must address the ego in all its glory. As I've mentioned before, every human component has two sides, the light and the shadow. The ego is not exempt from this conversation. It has a place in our lives but it's up to us to keep it in line and allow it to express itself appropriately. Give the ego an inch, it will most definitely take a mile.

Over the years, in different spiritual circles, I've heard people talk about how we need to quiet the ego or shockingly enough, how we need to kill it. Their take on it is that the ego is our greatest downfall, and it must be burned away like a wart in order for us to achieve the level of nirvana that that particular belief system has promised. And if you know anything about me by now, you can already guess that I emphatically disagree with them!

There is nothing wrong with having an ego. Having one is how we have stayed alive this long. Without it, you would have already died. It's precisely the ego that gives you the memory of when something hurts, the knowing that certain activities are dangerous, and the awareness of how far is simply too far. Without it, you would have already driven too fast into one-way traffic and off the cliff into the ocean. On fire. With scissors. Dead.

Through my own exploration into the topic, I have come to believe that the ego is where our human memories are stored. The ego records what has happened, filing the event away so that it's able to retrieve the data about what is safe and what is harmful. That way, the ego can calculate the safest route and protect the human. Essentially, it is our past-future projection, always computing what can happen based on what has already happened. Logic and reason come into play at this level as well, constantly collecting data for future prevention of harm.

Let's put it this way. The very first time you touched a flame, it hurt really badly, didn't it? Did you rush to put your hand in the fire next time you saw one? No. You remembered how much it sucked the first time. Your ego saved you from the second burn. Without it, you would have touch it over and over again, eventually just dying from total combustion. But it was your ego that stepped up, tapped you on the shoulder and said, "Hey, remember how that felt last time? Step away, or it will happen again."

Another lovely service the ego provides is the awareness of separatism and identity. How do you know you are you and not me? That's right. That little ego of yours is the knowing that you are there and I am here. It provides us with the experience of being our own self. Unique, special, individual selves! Without it, we would all be one big bubble of Divine Energy floating in space together. But with the ego, we can live our own life, eat our favorite foods, go to concerts to hear our favorite bands, and travel to our dream destinations. All because of that little tiny microchip in the brain called an ego. (And no I'm not talking literally…but since we are just biological programmable computers, it does kind of fit, doesn't it?)

With separatism comes individuality. From individuality comes identity. Our personality, quirks, skills, and talents is what makes us unique. We're all basically the same physical design, minus some external differences like skin, eye, and hair color. But the overall biology is the same. It's our identity that sets us apart. We give ourselves names. We wear certain styles of clothing. Maybe you wear makeup. Maybe your best friend doesn't. I like to color my hair. Perhaps you prefer your natural color. The beauty is in the little things. These contrasts set us apart from each other. And thank goodness for that! How boring would it be if we all looked the same?

So, why on earth would we want to kill it? It's not in your way. YOU are in your own way. The stories and programs that you believe, telling yourself that you aren't good enough or that you'll never succeed, *that* is what is in your way. The ego, in its perfect expression, isn't the cause of your failings. So stop vilifying it! Embrace it. Walk up to it and say, "Thank you, Mr. Ego. Thank you for saving my life and giving me an identity. Thank you for being a part of my wholeness." Do that first, and then we can talk about how it works against you and what you can do about it.

Shadow Ego

The light side of our ego works *for* us. It's supportive and proactive. It has a purpose and does its job well. When the ego is in check, it is in alignment with our Highest Good. The shadow ego, however, is what works against our alignment. It is the not-so-great attributes of humankind. Our job as conscious creatures is to know the difference between these two sides and to know from which one we are living. In light of that, I would be doing you a great disservice to talk only about the light side of the equation without also discussing its shadow.

This is a part of the human that isn't so great. While the light side of the ego is busy creating the space for you to feel special and unique, the shadow ego is secretly wanting to be superior and always striving to be right. Most often, being right at the cost of another. The only way it can be superior/right is to put someone in the place of being inferior/wrong. Aggressive competition, exerting power and control, and other domineering traits will come out in one's behavior when the ego is left unchecked. We will fight to the death sometimes for the thing we stand for. Blinded by our rage at the enemy, we will strike back at anything we perceive that is trying to make us wrong. This is the side of the ego that I'm not so much a fan of. This is the characteristic of humanity that can get very ugly, misguided, and eventually destructive.

It is where wars rage and violence is born. Judgment ensues and prejudices flare up. We vilify anyone who's different than us, whomever we perceive to be "less" so that we can be "more." We push and shove our way through life, trying to make people the example of "wrong" and build ourselves up to be crowned "right."

To look out into our communities and see differences in each other is natural. This is the beautiful design of a contrasting experience. And when the ego is in its light aspect that can mean acceptance of diversity and celebrating each other's uniqueness.

But the shadow ego wants to make anything that is different wrong. It wants to be in control of you by having you fight for its rightness. The human gets very attached to being the victor without any openness to see the other person's viewpoint. And what's worse, we will be willing to fight, even kill, for that status. It's dangerous, toxic, and destructive. Which is why we need to talk openly about it.

Superior vs. Inferior

Personally, this topic is one of my best checkpoints to just make sure I'm staying aware of myself and keeping my shadow ego at bay.

Anytime we are behaving from a place of being either superior or inferior to another, we are in our shadow ego. Let me repeat that. When you think of yourself as being better than someone else or lower than someone else you are standing smack dab in your shadow ego. Plain and simple. And since this can be a tricky game, I'm going to break down a couple of examples for you, showing you what is happening "behind the scenes" in each. I will put myself in both situations, inferior and superior, to give you an idea of how it plays out.

Myself in the Inferior Position: I have someone in my life that I admire greatly. I see many things in them that I wish I could be/do/have. Over time, I begin to put that person on a pedestal because I don't feel I can achieve whatever it is I see in them. This is the moment that I am placing myself in the inferior position. Outwardly, it appears that I am celebrating them in their accomplishments by exalting them. But secretly, I am shaming myself because I feel I'm not as good. When I look at that person, I see someone who is better than me. This is my shadow ego at play.

Subconsciously, I'll begin to project pressure and expectation onto that person so that they remain in that perfect status and never disappoint me. On some level, they feel that pressure. As time passes my resentment boils over, and I will kick the pedestal out from under them to "bring them down to my level." Obviously, this behavior isn't a conscious choice. It comes from a subconscious place where my emotional wounds lay buried and festering. Somewhere within me, I realize that I am in the lower position and will attack the very person I have lifted up, blaming them for pushing me down.

I see reporters do this all the time in Hollywood. One week, they are praising an actor for their amazing life choices, awards, and personal relationships. The next week the tabloids are digging up every skeleton in their closet to shame them. For some reason, we love to build others up and then kick them down again. It appears humans like to worship others but then instantly resent them because of their higher status, forgetting the fact that we had a hand in their rise to fame. It's a vicious shadow cycle.

If we constantly talk down to ourselves to stay in the inferior position, we will rarely take chances to achieve anything beyond our current situation. We won't feel worthy or safe because we've beaten ourselves down to the point of not wanting to risk judgment or failure. There tends to be a victim and/or martyr-type mentality accompanying this kind of behavior. Instead of being inspired to birth beautiful creations of our own, we'll shrink and allow the superior person to dominate (regardless if they are aware of it or not). We'll eventually blame the superior person for taking all the stuff we secretly wanted but didn't feel good enough to have. There is no possibility of alignment in this position.

Myself in the Superior Position: I am a talented person and my star is rising. People love me for the thing that I create in this world, and it feels good! I look down on others that wish they were me. Anytime another tries to do their thing I feel threatened, ridiculing their attempts to succeed. I want to be in the spotlight and they are a threat to the image I project. This is the game of being in the superior position.

To others, it may look like I am confident and proud of the work I've done. They may even be putting me on a pedestal themselves, which only exacerbates my inflated ego. Secretly though, I feel insecure and really don't believe in myself. I feel like a fraud and I'm afraid they're all going to find out. I attack my competition to cover up the fact that I don't feel secure in my abilities. For fear of being discovered, I must push down anyone who threatens my status within the community. It's bullying any way you slice it.

There is a very big difference between owning one's talents and being arrogant about it. Arrogance is the boasting of oneself while cutting down another. We exalt ourselves as being better than the rest.

It is the shadow ego coming out to play by negating beauty and talent in others in order to feel superior.

I believe that the counterpart to arrogance is confidence and conviction. That arena is where we can be proud of our hard work and can celebrate the value of our creation in the world. And yet, no one is being harmed in the process. We don't feel the need to kick anyone down in order to feel important. It's the ability to celebrate ourselves in our respective fields while simultaneously honoring the achievements of others. It's not competition, it's a joined celebration.

Regardless of the reasons we play these shadow games, we do it all the time. Sadly though, no one can ever win. When a person is pushed down enough times, they'll eventually feel they aren't valuable and will abandon their talent for fear of more harm coming towards them: It's best to just play small and stay safe. And the superior person may have "won the game." But do you think people are going to like hanging out with someone like that? Nope. In time, they will lose their true friends because people don't really like being bullied.

I'm not going to lie and feed you false comfort by telling you this is the easiest work you'll do in this book. The shadow ego is sneaky. You have to be diligent and catch that little bugger. We all feel insecure in certain areas of our life. We all look out into the world and cringe that someone else might be doing it better. Yet, there are moments when we feel indomitable. When we're the best in the whole wide world at that thing we just did. It's okay. No one's perfect. The goal is to simply be mindful. To watch from where you are choosing things and to witness how you are in action towards your people. To see your motive and be clear about it at any given time. Are you happy for your people when they accomplish something? Ask yourself, "Am I being either inferior or superior right now?" If you find that you are, ask yourself why. Dig a little bit in there and see if you can uncover the thing that you're trying to cover up. It's only when we dare to face the ugly side of our ego that we'll ever understand the whole of who we are. And when we can understand, we can heal.

Ask Better Questions

In the vein of asking questions, where are you in your own need for rightness? Are you attached to being right with people? Can you see times in your life where you just wouldn't back down, regardless if you were truly correct or not? Is there any wiggle room in those conversations to see the other person's viewpoint? It doesn't mean you have to change your mind and give in. That isn't what I'm talking about. I'm talking about being balanced in your rightness but not making others wrong while doing it – simply allowing them their rightness as well.

Yes, I may be a dreamer. I may look through rose-colored glasses at times. But dammit, I believe in a world where we do better than we're currently doing. I believe in the human, the spirit, and all the rest that mixes and mingles to make up who we are. Isn't it possible that each person has the right to be right? Isn't it okay to be wrong once in a while? And please understand – I'm not talking about morality and right versus wrong in a legal sense. We have laws to govern for a reason. There are some things in this world that are inherently wrong and must be legally enforced.

But in this context, I'm simply speaking of ideas, thoughts, opinions, and the way we express ourselves. It doesn't mean that we have to agree or follow suit. We can simply move away from that experience if we don't agree with it. That's what it's about, witnessing the contrast and deciding if you want to have it or not. I am me, and you are you. Do you have to like me? No. And I don't have to like you. But it's not a right or wrong situation. I don't have to push you down in order to feel superior. And I don't need anyone telling me I'm worthless just so they can feel above me. We can be strong in our own beliefs while honoring where someone is in theirs. Okay. I'll get off my soapbox now. But dammit, we can do better. And it starts with each one of us.

The Uncomfort Zone

I want to touch on one last component that the ego oversees. Going back to the point that the ego is responsible for our survival, there is a little, tiny thing worth mentioning. Remember we talked before about how the ego records all the past experiences so that it can project into the future? How it is calculating with logic and reason whether or not the direction you are about to go is a viable choice? Well, that sometimes gets in our way.

Yes, on a physical level, where mortality is in question, it's important to calculate safety. But what about all the other times in life when we are not in actual danger? Sometimes, the ego can't tell the difference between life threatening and uncomfortable. It perceives anything outside of that zone as dangerous and will do whatever it can to keep you safe. Even if that means sabotaging your future prospects and talking you out of amazing opportunities. It would rather have you sit still than risk your safety.

Any chance for a promotion at work that requires you to train large groups of people but public speaking is a requirement. Any moment where you are introduced to the person of your dreams, but you're afraid because your heart has been broken. All the times when adventure came knocking on your door and you didn't know what was going to happen, so you did nothing.

The comfort zone is a dream killer. It has the potential of sucking all the joy and passion from our lives. And it's the ego at the very center of it, telling you that it is too dangerous so you probably shouldn't risk it. It will talk you out of taking chances, trying new things, even putting your heart out for the world to see. It wants us to live a small life because it's able to calculate our safety to secure our survival. It can project the future much easier if you just sit still and be quiet. The ego is designed to keep the human alive, and sometimes it gets confused with what is actually going to kill us and what might just hurt our feelings.

Go back to when you were a kid and you found yourself in a very passionate game of tag. One kid was "it," the base was agreed upon, and the "running for your lives" would ensue. Remember how fun that was? I see our comfort zone being very much like base in a game of tag. Base is where you are able to catch your breath, devise a new strategy, and regain your composure. It's a pause in the adventure. Base was never designed for you to stay there forever. If kids did that, there would be no game. It's about the running off of base, the screaming and laughing, the almost-being-it. That's why we played it. For the fun of it. If all the kids stayed on base, it would be super boring. So, we run. We play. We come out of our comfort zone, knowing we can always go back to catch our breath. But the adventure resides within the game. Not on base.

As an adult, the goal is to be aware of your motives for choosing your experience. Is the danger real or is it perceived? Sometimes, asking better questions helps us get a little perspective, allowing us to shift our energy enough to choose what we want. And it's even acceptable to choose to stay comfortable if that's what you need at that moment.

But living a small life because you're afraid just isn't good enough. You know it. I know it. We weren't born in this life to be small. We were each given a powerful voice and a creative spirit. We have a fire in our belly that needs to burn with passion. Something within knows we are limiting the magnificent being that we truly are.

So, what if you put yourself out there, and some people don't like it? What if you have wonderful words to say and no one listens? Are you going to not say them? Who cares if someone doesn't get what you're trying to do. What matters is if you get it. What matters is doing it, living it, playing in the brilliance of this life. People will either get it or not. It's definitely a bonus when they do, but it shouldn't deter you from playing the game if they don't.

Higher Self

Now let's turn the tide a bit and talk about the spirit side of the total human. This is what we call the Higher Self (HS). It has a broader perspective of the total experience that the lower self (physical human) simply does not. Its vantage point is much higher, seeing the bigger picture where our ego sees only what it perceives right in front of it. The contrasting ego with its microcosm viewpoint is perpendicular to the macrocosm awareness of the HS.

I like to think of it as being the periscope to our submarine. The submarine (human) can better navigate the rough waters of life when it's able to get a quick look through the periscope (HS). Without it, we would be driving blind so to speak, hoping we don't crash into anything. And we've already covered what happens when we let the ego make all the decisions. Yet without the ego, our HS wouldn't know its individuality and have the physical experience. Really, this contrast is the perfect complementary relationship between physical and nonphysical.

Keep Climbing

There are three aspects of a human worth discussing at this point: The Higher Self, which helps us see the bigger picture in the hopes that we choose the direction that will best support our life. Next, we have the ego self. Our ego is uploaded with logic and reason to best calculate our survival. Its ultimate goal is to steer the human in the direction of least resistance and possible harm. And lastly, we have the free will human (lower self) who is the one in charge of making the choices in life. The free will human can take suggestions from the ego and HS, but ultimately they have the right to choose the direction to take. It truly takes a village!

HIGHER SELF PERSPECTIVE

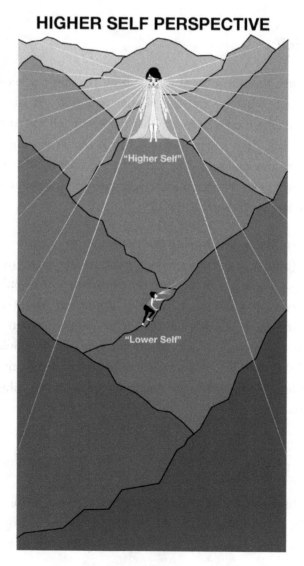

Let's face it, much of life can feel like we're climbing the rockiest of mountains with the most jagged path ahead. Dangerously scaling the wall, hoping with all our might that we don't tumble down the crags, we try to reach the top of whatever goal we have set for ourselves. It's both exhilarating to wonder what adventures lie ahead and exhausting to think of the energy it will take to get there. How are we to know if the steps we are taking are the ones that will support our best outcome? Good news is, we aren't alone in that journey to the top!

In the image to the left, the Higher Self (HS) has the greater vantage point, capable of seeing a full 360 degrees from the top of the mountain. As the human (lower self) is climbing their way through life, the HS is cheering them on, offering insights, support, and motivation to help them reach their greatest potential.

There are moments when the human will doubt, get frustrated, and possibly want to turn around and go back. This is the ego at work, wanting to survive and calculating that it is much too risky. In its limited vision, the ego cannot see the point of this journey. Because it cannot calculate the end result, it will see little value in allowing the human to continue. Without the aid of the HS, the human would probably get discouraged and not risk the climb at all. When the human is open to the guidance and chooses to follow the directions given, they are able to reach the top and see for themselves that it was indeed, worth it.

This is the relationship between the HS and free will human (lower self). In our daily grind, we rarely see beyond our perspective. Our viewpoint is limited and fear closes us off to possibilities beyond what we can comprehend. Our ego worries for the end result it cannot calculate safely and works ever-so-diligently to keep us quiet and in place. But our HS sees it all. It sees the point to the adventure. It has its finger on the pulse of why we are alive. And as an added bonus, the HS will guide us every step of the way to reach the top. We are asked to trust, keep going, and risk leaving our comfort zone in order to have our dreams come to fruition. No biggie, right?

Connection to Source

For clarification, the HS is not your soul, although both participate in the evolution of higher consciousness and beneficial navigation. The soul of each person is the essence that is eternal. It is the part of us that will live on after our physical body dies. Our soul is the one that plans the adventure for when it is on Earth in physical form. It writes the contracts and agreements with each person we intersect with during our life. It is the writer of the path before we're born, mapping out the goals and directives of the experiences it would like to have. This is where the main directive is created in the hopes that once the human is born and begins to exert its free will, the soul will have the full experience of its well-thought-out plan.

The HS is more like the navigator of the whole machine. It oversees the total experience and supports the decision making process, hoping to steer us towards the fulfillment of those directives. The HS may or may not live on. Some say it is directly connected to the soul. Others treat it as a temporary member of our committee.

I see it as a conscious pathway channel to Source. It is what guides us to make choices that keep us in alignment. And when we choose experiences that do not serve our Highest Good, it funnels data into our different guiding systems alerting us of such. The HS and the ego are on the same team, but on opposite ends of the spectrum. Where the ego is driven to keep the individual safe and sound, the HS is wishing the human to have an experience on a much grander scale.

When we have our ego in check, we generally want to move in the direction our soul set forth for us. But when these two sides are at odds, we sabotage our success, even if it is our true passion. The power of our shadow ego will nullify the desire of our soul and HS and have the human walk away from what is in their heart. This is why we feel disappointed when we've chosen to live small. Something in us knows we chose the safest route, but not the best route.

So Good!

Our soul is the component of our entire being that is in charge of choosing the path before birth. For me, the Highest Good is the direction that was intended. It is the collection of goals, contracts, and projected possibilities the soul came to this planet to work towards. Factor in the part about forgetting everything when we are born, add a plethora of free will choices, shadow ego, and all the fodder that they provide, well we've got quite the recipe for chaos. I'm not saying that's a bad thing. I'm just saying it can get pretty crazy when humans are running around frantically, trying to figure things out, all while trying to NOT DIE!

When I speak about serving the Highest Good, there are several moving parts to that conversation for me. I'm considering what my soul possibly wanted to have in that moment. I'm looking at my motives and keeping my shadow ego in check. I'll ask questions around any fears that might be bubbling up to the surface. I take into account the other people that might be involved and how my choices may affect them. And finally I look at my own integrity on the issue and double check where I am with the decision I'm about to make.

All of that might sound tedious, and probably and little bit of some over achieving. But honestly, it all funnels down in a singular moment where I ask, "Does this align with me?" I go by how I feel. It's that simple. If I feel what I am about to do is something that uplifts my spirit, excites my heart, and opens my energy, then I know I am in alignment with my HS. If what I'm considering is heavy in my chest, feels like something is oppressive around me, and my joy is sucked away, I don't do it. I know that if I choose to move forward, I will be choosing something that takes me out of alignment with my HS.

Cue the fun visual aid

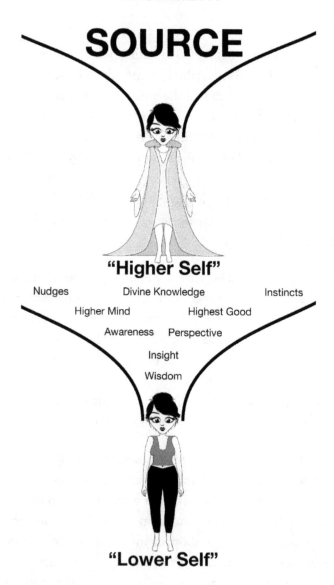

ALIGNMENT

SOURCE

"Higher Self"

Nudges   Divine Knowledge   Instincts

Higher Mind   Highest Good

Awareness   Perspective

Insight

Wisdom

"Lower Self"

When I talk of being in alignment with the Highest Good, often this is the imagery I see in my mind. Here we are at the bottom of our image, being human (lower self), living life, making choices, and doing our best to stay out of trouble. Above the physical human, we see the HS, who is directly connected to the wisdom that is available through Source. This is alignment in all its glory. It illustrates the wisdom funneling down from Source into the HS. This flows freely to the human as insights, intuitive hits, and overall awareness. When we cultivate this relationship, we are able to make choices that truly serve our Highest Good. We can better navigate the mine fields of life and take action to support the big picture – the soul's plan.

When we ignore these insights and nudges from our HS, we fall back into the habit of making decisions that will keep us safe. We slip out of alignment and into survival mode, allowing fear to be the dominant frequency. We have moved away from the Highest Good and are now listening to the ego. Which we've discussed, isn't always the best decision.

In earlier chapters I've talk about self-awareness and the importance of being present to your physical and emotional reactions. This is the map explaining why that's so important. When we are in alignment, we experience flow, ease, enlightenment, and joy. Misalignment causes rough waters, bumpy streets, and jagged-rocked journeys. Life is clearly harder when we live outside of this alignment.

Attached Much?

Another valuable topic of discussion is how humans get extremely attached to the outcomes we desire. Once we decide on the prize, everything in our being tries to will that end result. We want what we want, and we're willing to do just about anything to get it. In our minds, we have invested our whole reputation on having it. If it doesn't work, it'll reflect badly on our value in the world. From an ego standpoint, there is alot at risk. In order to keep that from happening, we will fight to our last breath to have it come to fruition, pushing and pulling in every direction, bending it to our will. As we've discussed in previous chapters, this is us, pushing all that we are out into the Universe, controlling the situation to our liking. This is another facet of the shadow ego wanting to be right, disallowing any space to have what is best.

In those moments, we are essentially telling the Universe that we know what would be best for us. We are not interested in any other options it might have. This is it. We've decided. In our infinite wisdom, we know best. (That's sarcasm in case that wasn't clear.) Knowing what you want is knowledge. That's the whole point of experiencing the full spectrum of human life. But, being willing to release your attachment and remain open to what is best, that's wisdom. The human part of us doesn't know everything, and yet often acts as if it does. It's our soul that has the plan. It has a trajectory in mind.

When we make choices that take us off of that trajectory, our HS gives us indicators that we've stepped out of alignment, letting us know we are no longer headed in the way that it was intending. That can show itself in a variety of ways. Discomfort, having that nagging voice inside, pain in the body, emotional upheaval, and chaotic thoughts just to name a few.

But when we are going in the direction that the soul initially stated, we get indicators that reassure us that we are in fact, headed the best way. Peace and ease, a sense of happiness and excitement, lightness in the body, and emotional/mental clarity are ways alignment can manifest.

I believe this is why we feel our choices. When we decide to do something that serves our Highest Good, it feels like a "Hell Yes!" The flow comes up from the upper belly, into the heart and out the throat.

It's what you might feel when you are inspired and elated. It's that rush when something is exciting, even if you don't quite see the end result.

Let's say you are inspired to take a brave step into the unknown, and you feel that rush of energy. But suddenly, the ego begins to talk you out of it, justifying the need to stay in place and not risk it. The feeling will result in a heavy, dense "fall" into the belly like a ton of bricks. The inspiration gets sucked out of you, and you are no longer inspired to move forward. It's in these moments, I try to remember a statement I heard years ago: the first answer is always the truth. The second, is your ego.

Every single minute of our day we are making decisions and calculating end results. Sometimes we get it right. Other times, we crash and burn. We aren't perfect, and there's no way we'll ever be. Good! Perfect is boring. Perfect isn't the point to having this human adventure. We are here to make choices, get messy, fuck up, try again, and figure it out. It's part of the Free Will Deal!

And I get it. It's scary to step into the unknown. We can't know for sure whether or not we'll succeed. We won't know if someone is down the road just waiting to jump out of the bushes and attack us. Our ego can't see that far. That's when we need to acknowledge the ego for the great job its doing, thank it for keeping us safe, but tell it to take a back seat. Because this life is to be lived. This life is our great adventure. All of it. The ups *and* the downs. We can't live our life never getting hurt. We are our greatest teachers when we fall down. When we muster the strength to stand up and try again, that my friend, that is what makes us. We are not made to sit on base, watching everyone else have fun. We were meant to play!

The Wisdom Within

I believe that within each of us a Divine Wisdom resides. I'm not talking about our intellect or logical reasoning. I'm talking about that part of us that just *knows*. It remembers what our great plan was before we were born even if we lack the conscious memory. It's the inkling that nudges us in the direction that our soul wanted to go before we ever stepped foot in human form. I believe this wisdom is radiated from our HS. Our various systems, guides, and even our own intuition are just tools the HS uses to help us connect to that wisdom.

In coaching sessions, I tell my clients on their first meeting with me that somewhere, at some point in our process, their wisdom will turn on and start driving our sessions. That something in them will ignite and begin to guide our journey. We may have an initial schedule of topics to discuss just to get us started. But eventually, we'll get insights on the true direction that will serve their overall Highest Good. And it's in that moment that we drop all attachments, and we go where their wisdom guides us.

We were all born with this innate knowing. As children, we had a stronger awareness of it, but we lacked the motor skills and language to fully express ourselves. Over time, life piled up onto us, coating, layering, and hiding this beautiful truth. This left us to live by obligations, appointed roles, expectations, and agreements, taking us far away from our own internal knowing. Part of my work is focused on removing those layers so that the wisdom can breathe a little, stretch its wings, and get back to its plan: Guiding humans towards their Highest Good.

My commitment to them is to hold a safe space, simply being present and remaining flexible for that particular moment. If I am attached to having the coaching go my way, then I am coming from my ego. I would be judging what I think they need and influencing the direction we go, all the while working really hard to be right about it.

Equally, if I let the client steer from their judgment, we are listening to their ego. But we wouldn't get a quality level of shadow work done because as I've said, the ego perceives anything uncomfortable as dangerous. And let's be honest, working in the shadow can definitely be uncomfortable.

One client came to see me because she wanted help healing from a betrayal in her family. She was so angry with her sister that the pent up anger was beginning to hurt her physically. She wanted the tools to be able to forgive and move forward. We set out on our journey together with that intention. A few sessions in, we realized she was a natural medium because her innate skills started "turning on" as we worked. This was a foreign concept to her so we shifted our focus to better support her gift while additionally giving her the tools to help heal her relationship. Her wisdom began to drive our sessions.

Another client wanted help in strengthening her psychic skills and was seeking the tools that would support her. Although, at some point we realized she had several past lives where she had been persecuted for having psychic abilities. The trauma of those experiences were being stored in her psyche, disallowing her to come fully into her gift. Her past lives were afraid that she too, would be persecuted, so they "locked up" her gifts so that she couldn't access them. Thinking they were protecting her, they were actually hindering her growth. Therefore, we shifted our focus a bit, provided some relief from her past wounds, giving peace to those lives, and opened the doors to her natural gifts. Her wisdom alerted us to the situation so that we could provide the complete healing she needed.

It could happen in the second session or the eighth. There really is no right or wrong moment, only that it awakens when it's time and when it feels safe enough to emerge. Inevitably, the wisdom will show us what is needing attention, what seeks to be healed in order for them to step more fully into their authentic self. Suffice it to say, it truly is the magick of the process. When their wisdom turns on, I know they are ready for what it has to offer. It is offering information of who they really are, not just who they think they are. Their resistance is minimal, their openness is peaceful. It just flows. No push, no pull, we just listen and trust. And follow.

My point in sharing these stories with you is to illustrate that we all have this potential of turning on our wisdom. Each and every one of us has within our whole being, a deep and Divine Knowing. It is unique unto us and is the truest connection to our wholeness. The wisdom is there. We've just been accustomed to covering it up, not trusting it, and pushing it down. But, bottom line is nothing can take the place of living in alignment with one's wisdom. Ever.

CHAPTER 9

Weave

We've made it to the last chapter! For those of you who didn't abandon ship, I salute you. I've lived enough years on this planet to pick up a few things here and there about humans. I completely understand how conversations like the ones in this book can be "earth shattering" for some. I'm daring you to question everything you have put in place to keep you warm and fuzzy. I'm inviting you to look at that blanket and ask if it really keeps you safe or does it just hide you from the monsters you perceive. We all put blinders over our eyes because the truth can sometimes be too painful. We don our robes. We play our roles. We try to fit in and go along with things because standing out and making noise can get us hurt.

And here I come, bouncing into your life with the mother of all snow globes…shake-shake-shake! Inviting you to unearth all that rests in the shadows, like silt in a pond. Out of sight. Out of mind. Silent. Safe. Shake-shake-shake! Daring you to look at yourself with a fresh set of eyes. Challenging you to be open to a new realm of ideas and possibilities. Shake-shake-shake!

Remember though, with the shake, also comes the stir. Something gets stirred within us when we seek a new vantage point. Something awakens in our psyche when we question all that we've ever known. We enliven from within when we ponder the possibility of taking off the blinders to see what's truly around us, not just accepting the painted version of someone else's perception of reality.

I once heard it described this way: You know what you know. You know things like driving a car and ordering a pizza. We know these things because we have probably experienced them firsthand. But you also know what you don't know. You know about brain surgery but more than likely, you don't know how to do it. You're probably aware of how helicopters work in theory, but there's a high probability that you don't know how to navigate one. There are many things in this world that we know exist but we lack the knowledge it takes to master them.

But what about the things you don't know that you don't know? This is where the mind boggles. I'm guessing that right now you're trying to think of something as an example. But whatever you come up with falls into the categories of the first two "knowings," purely because you have the awareness of them. Just for a moment, explore the possibility of the not-knowing space. That is where I'm asking you to be open to.

Hopefully, this conversation has already hit a few notes for you, and even though you may not have had the language around it, you're resonating with what I've shared. Or perhaps you stuck with it out of sheer spite just to be able to refute my claims that you are, indeed, a spiritual being having a human experience. Regardless of the reasons, the truth remains that you are still with me. I see you. I honor you. And I thank you.

Inspired Assignments

Now that we've discussed, in ample supply, the "what," let's talk about the "how." So many times, I see people get overwhelmed with information from teachers and mentors. They load their clients and students up with terminology, history, philosophy, and theory but don't finish up with practical application. What good is all that information if you don't know how to actually put it to good use in your life?

With that in mind, in this chapter, we'll spend some time weaving together all the beautiful facets, layers, and components that make up the spirited human. Just as a master clockmaker keeps the clock ticking, we shall likewise learn to keep our organic machine maintained and ticking. Every breadcrumb you reach out to take leads you closer to the whole human you've always been.

The exercises I'm going to share are ones I've used to help me stay centered and aware through the crazy roller coaster that is life. They are techniques that my Guys have shown me over the years, and I've grown quite fond of them. These are my basics. No matter what I'm doing, how much I think I know about the world, or how too-big-for-my-britches I get, these are always the ones I come back to. Some will resonate. Others may not. Just take what does and throw away the rest. Remember to be open-minded and give them a chance. It may not be that they don't work for you. You might just be butting up against your ego and resisting them. The mastery is in knowing the difference.

These exercises are meant to be a jumping off point just to get you started. We are all different, and what works for me may not work for you. It's completely acceptable to take these and adapt them to your liking. I'm very clear that I too, am an ever-learning being fumbling my way through life, trying to do my best. So I'm not attached to having you do it my way.

Baseline Reading

The most important step for any awareness exercise is to first be clear and present to how you are feeling in general. The foundation for any personal change first comes from the awareness of how you feel.

Without that information, how would you know change needs to occur? So, we start there. Baseline Readings (BLR) are a systems check scan. It is an overall snapshot in the moment of how you are doing. Taking that awareness into your day, so to compare new sensations as they arise. This way you are better able to determine if the new experience is something that you want to have or something that you want to walk away from. Knowledge is power.

I would suggest doing this five-minute exercise every day before jumping into the tasks, errands, and demands put upon you. Start by sitting in your favorite chair or in your meditation space, close your eyes, and breathe. Bring your awareness completely to yourself. Don't worry about your to-do list. It isn't going anywhere.

In your mind's eye, "run a scan" through your body, emotions, mind, and spirit, and make note of any insights, sensations, pain, and just the general state of your person. Are you rested or fatigued? Do you have a headache, or are you clear-headed? Is your heart particularly tender today, or do you feel strong and resilient? Are you connected and aligned, or do you feel disjointed overall? You're not necessarily doing anything about these awarenesses, you're simply acknowledging them. I strongly suggest keeping a notebook close by so you can jot these down.

Journaling throughout this process supports you in two ways:

1. As you compile the experiences, you will be able to go back and look for patterns. You may notice a specific time of day or daily event that puts undue stress on you. And ladies, you can also gain some clarity on your natural cycle and know better how to support your body's needs proactively.

2. It strengthens your self-awareness. The more proficient you become at scanning during the exercise the more you'll notice your awareness throughout your day. You are strengthening

that muscle. This gives you the ability to change course in the moment when you are experiencing something unwanted.

This is your baseline – the start point to your day. Keep in mind though: We're not going for perfect. Don't judge yourself if you feel a bit off. Don't flood your system with a false sense of positivity just to say you're happy. And please don't stuff anything down because you think it's a "bad" emotion. We're looking for where you are and how you feel. Perfectly, in that moment, just as you are. The goal is to simply be present to how you feel so that when life gets moving you can compare the new sensations to your start point. This gives you the power to identify what caused that change and if you would like to keep heading in that direction or make an adjustment.

I know this exercise might sound a little elementary, but think about it for a minute. How many times do you end up feeling so overwhelmed but can't figure out why? Or how often do you run yourself into the ground and not notice it until it has actually caused your body harm? This exercise is about strengthening your self-awareness in those moments when you would normally fall into mindless habits. Running a BLR in the morning provides you with a baseline barometer of how you're feeling. During the day, if something drastically changes in your energy, mood, or mental state, you can refer back to your baseline. It allows you to retrace your steps to try to figure out what caused the changes in your state and wobbled you out of your center. That way you can see patterns of behavior and can change your course before you are harmed. Without awareness, we'll just keep making the same choices mindlessly and wondering why we feel so crappy.

Checklist

I'm a firm believer that knowing your own personal energy level, what it needs, and how to care for it at any given moment is the key to living an empowered, spirited life. This technique is a staple for me. I use it at any point in my day or night if I'm feeling out of alignment and I'm not sure what caused it. Since we are ever-changing, ever-flowing beings, the answers won't always be the same each time you do this particular exercise. So as you go down your list of questions, your answers might spark new queries and take you in a different direction. Just be open. Stay inquisitive and let your wisdom show the way.

The checklist exercise is a list of questions that you would create, designed to bring you into a proactive state of awareness. It is the follow-up step after you've done your BLR and something has happened that has taken you out of your alignment. The intention is to put you into a more proactive role in your experience. Creating a checklist is one way to do that.

To better illustrate, I'm going to share with you a bit of how my own mind works when I'm doing this exercise. When I'm asking these questions, I am directing them to the appropriate layer of my four bodies or to the chakra that I feel is in distress. If I'm not sure where the disruption is happening, I close my eyes, breathe, and focus on hearing my internal wisdom. I may start by going through each layer/chakra and asking if it needs anything. Then, I carry it beyond my personal space to see if outside stimuli has affected me in some way. All the while asking my wisdom within for guidance.

Here's how it sounds:

(Notice something is off) → How am I doing? → How does my body feel? → Am I tired? Dehydrated? How's my blood sugar? When was the last time I ate? → Do I need a massage? → Is this emotional? → What do I feel? → Is this mine or someone else's? → Where am I in my menstrual cycle? → What phase is the Moon? → Have I been overworking? → Do I need to go for a walk? → What do I need right this moment to honor myself? → (To my heart) What do you need right now to feel honored and supported?

I keep asking questions in a rabbit hole type way until I zero in on what is going on. The true answers come from within and will not sound critical and judgmental. That is the shadow ego trying to have a hand in the process. Once I figure out the cause, I ask myself (all of myself) what do I need to feel supported. And then I simply do it. Without judgment. Without making any of it wrong.

If your body needs rest, go take a nap. If it needs chocolate, have it. If you need a vacation day, schedule it. Whatever it asks for, do it. This simple act of "having your own back" cultivates love and trust from within. Give yourself whatever you need to get into balance and back to your baseline start point. Again, this technique seems super simple, but so often we are caring for others or are so far into denial that we don't recognize when we are feeling out of sorts. Sometimes, we miss the simple things because we are distracted by the chaos and drama in our lives. By asking questions in this manner, it naturally draws our attention back to our center. Making this checklist your natural habit will cultivate awareness of self and bring you closer to a healthy relationship with the many facets of who you are.

Backtracking

One particular exercise that I feel is invaluable is the ability to backtrack to see where we might have lost our alignment. Being an Empath, I sometimes get so bogged down in other people's stuff that I get to the point where I don't feel like me anymore. I'll use this technique along with my checklist to help me better determine where I've gotten lost.

When I realize that my energy and/or mood has changed drastically from my BLR, and I've gone through my typical checklist questions, I follow up with some backtracking. For me, it isn't enough to know how I feel, I want to know what I did to put myself in that state. That way, if it comes into my experience again I can possibly make a better choice. Working like an investigator would on a criminal case, I retrace my steps to find the point where I lost my center. My goal is to find the split-second decision when I either said/did something out of character or didn't say/didn't do something that I now regret. Remember, this work is not about being critical for your choices. We're not uncovering these events so that you can shame yourself. We are embracing the whole experience while working to be a more conscious participant in the flow of life.

It sounds a bit like this:

(Notice emotion/energy shift) What am I feeling? → Do I remember feeling this when I woke up? (Consult my BLR notes) → When was the last time I remember not feeling this way? (Go back in time) → What happened in that moment? (Slowly move forward to watch that event) → Did I say something that might have hurt someone? → Did I allow someone to hurt me without realizing it? → Is this emotion mine or did I pick it up from someone else? → What do I need to do to honor myself right now?

Go back until you find the last place where you remember feeling great. This might mean going back hours, days, or even longer to figure it out. We are known to carry things around with us until we break. So, be patient as you backtrack.

Once you find it, start to move forward in time and try to pinpoint the moment something happened that changed your mood. Did you

186

talk to someone? Were you rude to them? Did someone insult you and you ignored your boundaries? Did you watch the news or hear a report that hurt your heart? If you can find the moment your mood changed, you can take the necessary steps to start your journey back to your center. If you find that it was someone that hurt you, now you can clean up your boundaries with them. If you realize it was something you did, now you know where you need to take responsibility.

Give yourself whatever you need to feel supported and aligned. Be gentle with yourself during this process. Each time you do this exercise, you'll get better at catching it. And then one day, you'll be in the moment, and you'll see it happen in real time, giving you the chance to correct the issue immediately rather than later.

Clean It Up

This one is really a subcategory to the backtracking exercise. It's one thing to backtrack and discover someone hurting your feelings. But it's an entirely different situation when you realize you are the one at fault. We're not perfect. We are going to do and say things that are rude and off-color. We will hurt people's feelings, sometimes knowingly, and other times, by accident. This segment isn't about shaming you. I'm not going to get self-righteous with you because I've been known to put my foot in my mouth more times than I'd like to admit. It's real talk about real life. It's about taking responsibility for our actions and inactions. By having accountability for our choices, we're able to reclaim our integrity and put ourselves into a powerful spirited state.

I wholeheartedly believe that my alignment with my own integrity is the only thing that matters in this world. It is the central foundation from which every other aspect will either be strong or weak. My choice. When I strive for that alignment, I love myself more. I feel valuable, and I'm a better person to be around. So, that means taking a good, hard look at the times when I'm a jerk. And when I find those moments, my integrity demands accountability. I must do what it takes to put myself back into the good standings with my own alignment. Or my life just doesn't work. No, it isn't easy. It sucks big time to have to go to people I love and show them my dirty laundry. But when they forgive me and we move forward, our relationship is stronger and they trust me a bit more than they did before. And that I wouldn't trade for the world.

Or, let's say you backtrack and see that someone hurt you, but you allowed it without speaking up in your own defense. This will equally harm your alignment with your integrity because you let it happen. You'll end up projecting resentment onto the person when really you are mad at yourself for allowing the behavior. Either way, it's begging to be cleaned up. That's why it's so hell bent on getting your attention. *wink*

Exercise: Imagine you are standing at the fork of a road with several lanes. Each road represents your options in a particular situation. I'll use an example, one that I've run into a few several hundred times in my life. My best friend keeps cutting me off in mid-sentence. I allow it to happen each time, but it really hurts my feelings. Once I've backtracked and found the issue, and I'm clear I'm not okay with it happening, I start asking myself questions.

This is how that might sound:

I ask my heart: What are my options? (Sometimes I even write these down on paper)

Option A: I could let it go. She probably had a bad day and just needed to vent. (Even though it happens every time.)

Option B: I could wait until it happens again and then say something I've prepared, to let her know that I don't like being cut off.

Option C: I could call her on the phone and tell her it hurt my feelings.

Option D: I could break up with her and never talk to her again.

With each option, I am focusing on my heart, emotions, and physical sensations for clues to which one feels the best. I'm not asking my brain because it will more than likely want me to take the easy road and do what will keep me safe. I ask my heart, "What do you need to feel like we've cleaned this up?" And then, I notice the feelings as I speak the options out loud. When I feel a "yes," that's the one I do.

For instance, if I feel Option B is the right answer, I would prepare what I want to say before it happens again. I spend some time getting clear how it makes me feel and the words I want to speak to convey my truth without harm. Using this same "fork in the road" style of questioning, I ask my heart what it wants me to say to my friend next time.

Option A: Look bitch! That hurts! Don't do that again!

Option B: Man, are you ever going to let me talk? (A more passive aggressive approach.)

Option C: Sweetheart, I'm not sure if you know this, but when you cut me off like that it really hurts my feelings, and I start thinking you don't care about my viewpoints.

Option D: It's okay. I don't have much to say anyway.

Asking my heart, it would probably choose Option C. So, I practice what it sounds like and wait for the next opportunity. Then, I speak my truth without harm. Next, I shut up and wait for her response. That will tell me everything about my friendship with this person, and I can go from there.

Regardless of the end result, this isn't about the other person liking the fact that you want to clean it up. It isn't about their understanding or even agreeing with how you feel when you speak your truth. It is about you, your alignment, and your integrity. It's about giving your heart the message that you have its back, and you will take care of it. It's all about that relationship first. In the end, nothing else matters but how you feel about the person you are. And as we've said before, if your people love you they will want to support you. So it isn't an exercise in asking for permission to have boundaries. It's about renegotiating the relationship in order to move forward in the way that supports you both.

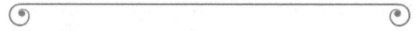

Sitting in the Mud

A common practice for humans is to designate a value to the contrasts we experience. Where having the awareness of the contrast can be an amazing tool in the quest to know self, it too can have a shadow side if we're using it to place judgment. We have within us a silly little program that feels the need to denote a value for the people, places, and things we interact with on a daily basis. Filing them away into two main categories: good/right and bad/wrong. This conditioned thinking is a prime source of our human pain. It limits our possibilities because we're too busy categorizing things in our limited perception. It boxes us into the pressures of trying to be good in order to be valuable humans. And we punish ourselves, sometimes our whole lives, for mistakes we made because it is a bad thing, therefore has no value.

We are told over and over again, in various ways, that we should always be happy, that having negative emotions means we are bad, and something is wrong with us. So, we work ourselves to death trying to stay happy at all times, living a lie, and keeping up the pretense just so others will look favorably upon us.

But as we all know, human life is in constant flux, with emotional hills, peaks, and valleys. We place so much judgment and criticism on ourselves for not being able to maintain these unobtainable emotional constants. Our very own heartbeat illustrates this perfectly. With every beat, the needle rises and falls. Perfectly, the beat of life. If it were a constant tone, it's what we would call a flatline, and we would be dead.

Why does having emotions have to be wrong? As we've discussed, emotions are navigational beacons letting you know how you're doing in life. They offer insights to your experience, allowing you to make corrections along the journey. They are not bad. They are extremely valuable.

The first thing we need to do is to have an open-hearted discussion about allowing yourself to feel. Sounds simple, right? But is it? Can you just let the feelings flow, without hindering them, without judging them and trying to push them down? Do you even know you do that? Most people aren't aware of the proficiency they have in pushing emotions deep down into their guts. That way, the feelings are truly out of sight and out of mind. So, we start by simply giving ourselves permission to feel whatever we are feeling at any given moment.

I call it "Sitting in the Mud." When you experience something that you judge ugly, wrong, or anything else with a negative connotation, you are rejecting it. And anything that you reject, you simply cannot receive nutrition from. You will disallow any messages that moment has for you and ignore any nutrition it might be offering for your own growth. So, rather than pushing it away and acting like you don't see it, sit in it. Feel it. Run it through your awareness and witness it. Have it all over you. The good, the bad, and the ugly. There is no judgment. No condemnation. No push or pull. Just observe and allow it to wash over you.

The very act of acknowledging that emotion already starts the process of healing. By witnessing it and not pushing it aside, you are allowing its validity, relaxation, and flow. By receiving it you are giving it value. And everything in this vast Universe just wants to be acknowledged. Your emotions aren't any different. Feel what it has to offer, as if you are amazed with curiosity and wonder.

Perhaps at this point you could ask the emotion some questions:

What are you? → Why are you here? → Is there something you want to teach me about my experience? → Why haven't you left? → Am I keeping you captive? → What do you need to feel at peace?

Pause between each question, and gently tune into yourself. Stay present to all that you are, and invite the answers to come. You'd be amazed what you can hear when you're truly open to receive. And sometimes, there is no message. Sometimes, the only thing the emotions need is to have you witness them. Just by being present and acknowledging what you feel, you have validated your emotions and honored your heart chakra. It is in that moment of being present that your emotions can begin to heal.

Be brave, stay open, and receive the nutrition that this process has to offer. You have beaten them into the ground long enough. That isn't working. It's time to try a new tactic.

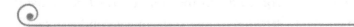

Food for Thought: Can you feel "bad emotions" and still be in alignment? Yes. This is the misconception of some spiritual teachings. There are many teachers, gurus, and coaches in the world that promise a constant state of euphoria if you do what they are telling you, buy every product they've ever made, and solemnly swear allegiance to them for eternity. And when you don't experience that state of bliss – because we're human and we have bad days – they'll claim that you are doing it wrong and need to try harder. This sets you up to judge yourself harshly anytime you feel anything on the not-so-great end of the emotional scale. Even a mundane case of melancholy isn't acceptable in most spiritual circles. We put on the fake happy face in front of our teachers because we don't want to be shamed for being bad students. It's too much pressure. Just stop!

Your alignment is not dependent upon your emotional state. Navigating your life based on your emotions is a valuable tool to have, but we're not striving to be happy 24/7. That's not realistic. And frankly, sets you up for failure because we cannot achieve that level and stay sane. Your awareness of your emotional state and how you care for yourself is what supports your alignment. Feeling the feelings is human. What you do in support of those feelings is mastery. If you hate your emotions, that's your shadow ego judging yourself for being wrong. So yes, you can be sad and still be a good person. As long as you give yourself permission to be so.

Wound Care

One of the most delicate and vulnerable techniques of shadow work is providing wound care to the pieces and parts that need it. We spend much of our time covering up our wounded areas with denial and avoiding these conversations. Like in the story of *The Princess and the Pea*, you keep adding mattresses so that you can get comfortable. But nothing works. Why? Because you can't cover up your wounds. They need to be cared for. I'm inviting you to take the mattresses off so you can finally rest.

And I'm not going to lie to you. It takes time, practice, and a lot of courage to do this work. It's not for the faint of heart. But it is oh-so-worth-it if you do! Like many of our exercises in this chapter, you'll need to adjust your language to personalize it for your needs. Also keep in mind the questions will change depending on the scenario. With all of the foundational work in the previous chapters, you've got a stable base for this step. Trust yourself. Trust the process. As always be gentle, stay focused, and try your best.

Here's how it might look:

- You've witnessed an event that doesn't involve you, and yet is extremely uncomfortable. It has triggered something within you, and you feel traumatize. Realizing that you may be overreacting because what is happening isn't happening directly to you, start by simply acknowledging your feelings. (If it is harming you directly, this is a boundary infraction and you will need to go another route.)

- Ask yourself questions that might dig in a little beyond your current field of vision. It can sound like: That's a really strong response. I wonder why? → What emotion am I feeling? → Is it mine or am I feeling someone else's? → What's really going on within me? → Why am I reacting this way? → Is there something I'm missing that needs my attention?

- I will actually put my hand on my heart and close my eyes for these questions. Be gentle with yourself. Ask the questions honestly with openness for the true answer, not just the quick cover up so you can move on. (That's the kicker!)

- The first immediate answer is usually the obvious one. It's the real-time, surface-level reason we are reacting. It might sound like a projected judgment towards the person you are witnessing. Or perhaps, it's the knee-jerk answer given in defense to being uncomfortable. That isn't the real answer, but it's an important start.

- Ask then, "What's under that?" Meaning the obvious answer is usually covering something that is even more tender, more vulnerable. Again, be gentle and take your time. Notice any sensations, feelings, thoughts, or sudden memories. What comes to mind? The second answer is still not the wound, so take what it is, but keep asking. This is the layer where we want to justify our behavior and excuse ourselves from taking ownership for our part in it. Our mind is seeking the nearest exit because it knows it's about to get uncomfortable. Press on, gently, but intently.

- Ask again, "What's under that?" Move gently in this area of questioning. Try to open your mind and allow any memories to come. It might be an obvious answer or something that you have forgotten years ago. You might not even get an answer, that's okay too. Remember, we're not looking for exact instances. We're looking for the same energy and emotion of the trauma. Keep your focus on the overall intention: finding what is wounded. Let it tell you where it is, and what it is.

"In a futile attempt to erase our past, we deprive the community of our healing gift. If we conceal our wounds out of fear and shame, our inner darkness can neither be illuminated nor become a light for others."
- Brennan Manning, Abba's Child: The Cry of the Heart for Intimate Belonging

---

I have found that there are typically three layers in wound care:

> *The obvious hurt* – what is right before your eyes and why you are reacting – the present situation – surface level

> *The secondary hurt* – what the obvious hurt is covering up that happened in the past – similar reaction/energy, but not always the exact same situation – under ground level

> *The original wound* – the initial hurt underneath them all, where the other hurts originate from (the pea) – again, similar energy but not always the same situation – core level

Side Note: We think the situations must match in order to find the pattern and heal the hurt. If a different person punched you in the face every single time, it would be easy to spot your wound. Done!

But life is random and it comes at you in many different ways, flavors, and styles. Instead, what you're looking for is the patterns of energy and/or emotion each time you are hurt. When you carry around a wound from the past, experiencing anything even remotely similar to that initial event will re-ignite the pain – much like the examples given when we discussed triggers and PTSD. Try not to fixate on the actual experiences matching and instead look for patterns of emotion. For example, Don might have punched you in the face in high school, but a few years later Sally slapped you. Later down the road, you could have been involved in a breakup where no physical violence was carried out at all. And yet, all three events felt the same and caused you to react as if you had been punched each time. The wound has nothing to do with the physical encounters, it's about the emotion stored up when the first altercation took place. And going even further down, it's about to story you believed about the originating wound that ignites the future hurts. Find the pattern of energy and you'll find the wound.

Once you get to the "pea" provide wound care. Much like you would for a physical cut, care for your emotional cut:

- **See the wound:** Acknowledge, witness, see it, and be with it (no judgment, no shame). You'll want to be gentle here. Adding any type of criticism will only deepen the wound. This isn't the time to get into who is right or wrong, or who is to blame. Be as gentle with yourself as you would if you were walking up on a wounded baby deer.

- **Clean the wound:** Love it. Apologize to it. Promise you will care for it. Commit to being its protector and healer. Have its back going forward and let it know it is safe now.

- **Flush it out:** Ask the wound what it needs. Let go of anger, fear, shame, guilt, etc. Whatever it needs to be at peace. This may take time. Allow all that you need without any time constraints or expectations. The goal isn't to hurry up and be done with it. The goal is to allow its own timing for proper healing while also not avoiding and being in denial.

- **Dress the wound:** Use proactive words of how you will care for yourself moving forward. Review your own responsibility and see how you can implement boundaries in the future. Backtrack and see where you might be allowing that same pattern in your life, and set up checkpoints that support you in making better choices. Remember, this is not the time to judge. I cannot state that enough! Review is NOT so that you can beat yourself up for the shoulda, coulda, wouldas. That will only reignite the wound and worsen its condition. This is about being proactive and empowered as you step forward, daring to embrace life.

Memory Lane: To further support you with this process, I'd like to share with you a story about my own wound care. It's a bit long, but I'm hoping it will give you an example of how the process works. A few years ago, a friend and I decided to do readings and healings at a music festival in Idaho. We shared a tent, decorated it with our goddess scarves and twinkle lights, and looked forward to a fun weekend ahead.

During this two-day event, a young girl would visit our tent every hour or so. She was obviously curious and wanted information about being intuitive. Her mother came over at some point and seemed to want to discourage her from walking that path. She would say things that were insulting and condescending towards her daughter, and quite frankly, to us as well. I didn't like her mother, and I refused to talk to her the whole first day. It would infuriate me every time I saw her.

In my head, I was better than she was. I was judging her for being a bad mother and would go into a silent rage each time she came to our tent. I was like a rabid dog, mentally attacking her for how she treated her daughter. At some point during the second day, after having been enraged once again, I realized that perhaps I needed to do some wound care. So, I began to dig.

I started the process by determining my judgment: She was a bad mom. This is the conclusive thought I had been projecting all weekend. So, then I looked at myself. Where have I been a bad mom? I knew I had "mom issues" from my own mother, but the reactions I was having didn't feel like they were attributed to her. This felt more personal. I kept digging.

I justified my mothering skills to myself, saying I would never treat my son like that. I would never insult him for wanting to learn teachings that were different than my own. For a long while, I just couldn't make the connection. My mind raced to find the answer while I kept chewing her energy up with my judgment.

Then, it hit me. I was a stepmother before I became a mother. In that time of my life, there was so much pressure to do well. I felt my husband's family looking down on me, just waiting for me to screw up (whether it was real or perceived). My whole life I had wanted children, so I was also putting pressure on myself to be the best I could be. I wasn't getting the support from my then-husband anytime my stepson and I butted heads. My husband would take his side and blame me for the fight. I was frustrated, angry, and afraid. And I didn't do a very good job. I wanted to be the best mother, but I feel I failed.

Click! There it was. I was harboring hatred, judgment, and sorrow for my own failings as a stepmother. And then when this woman showed up, outwardly being nasty to her child, it showed me the wound and how I felt about myself. My reaction had nothing to do with her. It was all my own shame I had buried deep within.

As I sat there, reeling from this new ah-ha, crying and feeling really crappy, I began the "cleaning it up" phase. I sent my stepson love through the ethers, asking his Higher Self for forgiveness. I forgave myself for my failings (perceived and real). And I sent the woman love for chewing her up like a dog's bone that whole weekend. I allowed myself to release all of the emotions, judgments, shame, and hatred I had been unknowingly harboring. Miraculously, the very next time the mom came over to our tent, I was able to talk with her, to walk her through her own misgivings about being psychic and helped her better understand her daughter's ability. All without being triggered. That is the power of wound care.

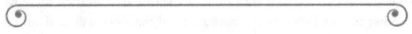

Each time you do this for yourself, you get better and better at the process. Your instincts sharpen, and your awareness heightens. Being proactive begins to build trust within yourself again and you regain alignment with your integrity. Somewhere you know you have your own back. This will then support other areas of your life the more confident you become. Remember to be gentle and do this work lovingly. Trust the wisdom that you are. It knows the way. The key is being in the questions, being open to what answers come, and being willing to let yourself heal.

Now What?

I know what you're probably thinking. What the heck do I do with all of this information? Am I right? I'll tell you the same thing I tell my clients. Take your time. Baby step each layer of magnificence that you are. There is no need to rush, force, or pressure yourself to achieve anything. This is not about the quick fix end results. Yes, it's great when we feel better and can see the benefit from doing this kind of work. But it's not a race. If you push through the pages of this book just to say you did it, you'll miss the whole point. Checking the boxes off doesn't mean you walk away with a stronger sense of self.

The point is about getting to know who you are. Who you *really* are. On a brand new level than ever before. The ins and outs of what makes you different from everyone else. You are re-educating yourself on how to care for your heart and mind. You are taking a bold step towards honoring the brilliant machine your body truly is. And you are inviting your consciousness to get reacquainted with your soul. That is no small undertaking.

It will take time. There will be days when you're so on fire with passion that every cell in your body is electrified. And then there will be other times when you are frustrated and the work will be daunting. So my advice: Run when you're able to. Walk when you can. And rest when you need. Any step forward is still progress. Even the baby steps. They are still taking you forward.

You've got this! I know you do! I'm a firm believer that there are no mistakes. For whatever reason, you have picked up this book. And if it wasn't a conversation that was intended for you, it would have never intersected your path. Our guides are magnificently creative. They have brought you to this moment in time, given you the information you need, and marvel at the adventure that awaits. What will you do with it? Well, that is completely up to you. That is the power you hold within your experience. To do or not to do. That is a beautiful question.

Be spirited, my friend!

Be brave! Be bold!

Be YOU!

Breadcrumb Trail

Did you think we were done? Oh no, we are only getting started! At the 11th hour, and because my guides usually like to surprise me when I'm least expecting it, there is a tasty treat waiting for you beyond these pages. I've created, solely for my readers, a video chapter explaining a final inspired assignment.

This particular exercise was given to me by my Guys in the early years of my business. At first glance it appears overly simple and you might be tempted to pass over it. But as I learned through the years of offering it to my clients, as well as using the technique myself, I found it to be deliciously revealing. We're all searching for the same thing. To know thyself. And this assignment offers a glimpse into the whole of all that you are. My hope is that it supports you on the journey into the world as a spirited human.

Here are the breadcrumbs to find the Bonus Chapter:

1. Go to www.morrighanlynne.com
2. In the "Author" section, click "Bonus Breadcrumb"
3. Enter "BeSpirited" for the password (case sensitive-no space)
4. Embrace what it offers, expand your heart and mind, and enjoy the game!

There will also be forms you can download to use along with the exercises laid out in the video. See you on the flip side! ♥

Glossary

Listed here are some of the terms I use not only throughout my book but in my daily life. I figured in order to fully support your journey through these pages you might as well have a glimpse inside my head and take a peek at my everyday terminology.

Archangels: an angel of high rank. The word "archangel" itself is usually associated with the Abrahamic religions. However, stories and artwork depicting beings that are very similar to archangels are found in a number of religious traditions. In my understanding archangels tends to be the "managers" of the various angelic realms that oversee humanity. They are specialists in that each have specific talents, abilities, and responsibilities that can assist and support humans in their daily lives.

Aura: see Four Body System

Authentic Voice: the outward creative expression that rises from the authentic self (the sacred being we were at the moment of birth); it is that place within us where the Divine Soul is expressed through our human self. We don't need to construct our words from thought when communicating this way. It is already aligned with our Highest Good and naturally flows in perfect expression.

Brain Speak: a term I use to illustrate when we communicate from a place of being calculative, methodical, and safe; we speak from the brain rather than the heart. We are choosing just the right thing to say that will have us be accepted and received by our peers.

Centering: the act of connecting the crown chakra to the Universal Energy/spiritual plane to stabilize, nourish, and align our spiritual essence with that of Divine Energy.

Chakra: Sanskrit word meaning "wheel". Translated from the Hindi meaning "wheel of spinning energy." It is a whirling, vortex-like, powerhouse of energy. There are seven main chakras within the physical body and thousands of minor ones within the body and aura.

Chakra System: the seven main chakras within the physical body that run from the tailbone to the top of the head. (I like including the ear chakras, but that's just me.)

Christ Consciousness: the highest state of intellectual development and emotional maturity. It is the state of awareness of our true nature, our higher self, and our birthright as children of God/Source.

Core Story: the stories that were given to us as children, typically negating programs that break down the self-esteem and inner value. As we mature we continue to carry these stories around, allowing them to cultivate and craft the adult we become.

Cosmos: the Universe regarded as a complex and orderly system; the opposite of chaos.

Divine Energy: having the nature of or being a deity. Of, relating to, emanating from, or being the expression of Source. Superhuman; godlike. It is the energy of the highest vibration and it is available to all.

Divine Tapestry: the tapestry in which all is woven upon. Each person, the timing of events, the order in which they occur, the perfection of each intersection, and how they relate to and affect one another; the macrocosm of all that exists.

Divine Wisdom: traditionally used to describe the wisdom that resides in God. I, however, personally believe we are all of God

(Spirit, Source, etc.), therefore I use this term to mean the wisdom from our Higher Self that is channeled directly from Spirit.

Dogma: a principle or set of principles laid down by an authority as undeniably true.

Earthbound: a deceased human's spirit that is still attached to the physical plane. They are "bound" to the material world and have not yet crossed into the spiritual realm.

Ego: the self especially as contrasted with another self or the world; a person's sense of self-esteem or self-importance.

Emotional Guidance System: Using your emotions to guide you through life; trusting your emotions to navigate you towards what will best support you; tapping into the wisdom your emotions hold and allowing them to direct you.

Empath: A sensitive person with the paranormal ability to collect the mental and/or emotional state of another individual; able to "read" information that others aren't able to detect. They have the capability of feeling emotions, vibrations, and environmental subtleties that others cannot feel.

Four Body System: the energy field that surrounds the human which is comprised of multiple layers. Each layer has a specific purpose that supports the overall experience of the human. Also called the aura.

Grounding: the act of connecting the root chakra to the planet/physical plane in order to secure and nourish the human essence and provide a sense of stability in one's life.

Guidance Team: the Divine Beings that are assigned to you through a contractual agreement, committed to guiding and supporting you throughout your life. Some are with you at the time of your birth and will stay until you cross over into the spirit realm. Others can come and go based on your immediate needs and requests. They are, but not limited to, angels, spirit guides, archangels, ancestors, guides specific to certain paths (Shamans, Druids, Celts, etc.), deities from different paths (Isis, Apollo, Freya, etc.), and totem animals.

Higher Self: a term associated with multiple belief systems, but its basic premise describes an eternal, omnipotent, conscious, and intelligent being. It is the part of our whole being that is directly connected to Source and can support our decisions in life through guidance.

Highest Good: traditionally a term used to note the good that is shared and beneficial for all (or most) members of a given community. I use it to further explain how as a human, we make choices every day that satisfy our ego but not always in support of the greater good. Our soul has an overall goal for this life. It wanted to have certain experiences that would further its awareness of itself. To choose things in support of our HG is to be in alignment with the trajectory of our soul's plan.

Ideology: a system of ideas and ideals, especially one that forms the basis of economic or political theory and policy.

Intuition: the ability to understand something immediately, without the need for conscious reasoning or evidential proof.

Lower Self: a term I use to explain the ego based human; the free will choice maker; the part of us that is incredibly reactionary with survival based instincts.

Macrocosm: the whole of a complex structure, especially the world or Universe, contrasted with a small or representative part of it. The big picture.

Magick (Magickal): it is a personal choice of mine to spell this word in this manner. Since I have been on a magickal path for over 20 years I choose to use the "k" to show and differentiate my personal path from that of performance magic.

Medium: a person claiming to be in contact with the spirits of the dead and to bridge communication between the dead and the living.

Microcosm: a community, place, or situation regarded as encapsulating in miniature the characteristic qualities or features of something much larger. Smaller, more immediate picture.

Psychic: relating to or denoting faculties or phenomena that are apparently inexplicable by natural laws, especially involving telepathy or clairvoyance.

Saboteur: a person who deliberately destroys, damages, or obstructs (something), especially for political or military advantage. I use this term to demonstrate when one harms their own life in order to stay small and play safe.

Sacred Observer: the aspect of the spiritual human that is capable of watching the lower self make choices, have experiences, and in general, live their life. It is the higher awareness, watching and witnessing, but is not attached to the outcome. See Higher Self. For contrast see Lower Self.

Shadow: based strongly on the works of Carl Jung, it is a psychological term for everything we can't see in ourselves. Typically it is the aspects we don't like about ourselves, therefore we hide them away so that others will not see our shame. Because one tends to reject or remain ignorant of the least desirable aspects of one's personality, the shadow is largely negative. There are, however, positive aspects which may also remain hidden in one's shadow if we believe we are unworthy of having such virtues. (Especially in people with low self-esteem, anxieties, and false beliefs).

Source: equally and simultaneously a deity and a location for me. It is the place in which we come from and the place we will return to once our physical body dies; synonymous with God, Goddess, Spirit, The All, Universe, etc. The label you choose to use is personal, I subscribe to all possibilities.

Spirit: (Divine as opposed to a human spirit), see Source

Star Person (Incarnate): a person that is currently human but their soul origin is from another planet, star system, or galaxy. Some call them Star Seeds, Star Children, & Travelers. They often have a difficult time assimilating as a human being because it isn't their true origin.

The All: see Source

Theology: The critical study of the nature of the divine.

Universal Energy: In Chinese medicine it is the term for the energy that permeates everything around us. It applies to the energy inside your body, as well the energy inside and outside any man-made structures. It is the energy that is available to all.

Woo-woo: descriptive of an event or person embracing New Age theories such as energy work, crystal magic, Reiki, or supernatural/paranormal/psychic occurrences.

Acknowledgments

First and foremost, I want to thank my husband, Jonathan. Without your love, patience, and belief in me I would not be the person I am today. You took this broken, wild thing and gave her the space and time she needed to trust that she could be safe. You left her wild, but now she knows how to love and can be loved in return. Thank you my one, for all you've done. Not only have you supported me emotionally throughout the process of birthing this book, but you were implemental in the structuring, technical aspects, and business functions that I simply have no talent for. You are amazing! I love you my Gnome. You and me baby! #929

Thank you to those that had a direct hand in this creation. To Keith Allen Kay, you took my ethereal words and concept and you gave her form. The art breathes because of you! Thank you for your gift. Angie Millgate, I don't know how you brought so much spunk and fire to the illustrations, but M'lynne is the perfect avatar for the lightheartedness of this book. And yet you can feel the strength in her journey. You rock sister! To my editor, Buffy Naillon, I deeply appreciate your patience and mentorship during this process. Being that this is my first baby, I was incredibly nervous and at times overwhelmed. But you were amazing! You walked me through all the steps and educated me on the process. I couldn't have done it without you. Alisha Newcomer, you were the very first one to witness what I was attempting. I was so nervous to have my words read by another living human! Your feedback and support mean the world to me. I love you! Lynnette Spurrier, thank you for taking the time to comb through the pages and polish her up. I needed fresh eyes after months of words swirling in my head. Your help is deeply appreciated! Now I feel confident to show her off.

I want to thank any and all that have loved me through the years. Those that showed up in my life and offered me the opportunity to learn from you, to learn with you. Thousands of classes, readings, and coffee dates. All the times we've have shared space, words, and love. I hope you can see yourself in these pages. You have molded me into the teacher and coach I am today. Watching you, working with you, living life and walking the path next to you…you are my mentors, my healers, and my shamans. I am forever grateful for you!

And if we're doling out gratitude for the growth I've experienced in life, I realize I must thank those that have hurt me as well. The ones that broke my heart and ripped me open. If it weren't for you I wouldn't know myself the way that I do. You broke open the false shell that was hiding my shadow. You cracked open all the pretense that I was hoping people would accept. I was lying to the world, to myself, in the hopes that I would be loved and accepted. I was playing the game just like everyone else. Because you denied me love I was able to love myself. Because you betrayed my trust, I learned to trust my own heart. If you hadn't rejected me I might not have gotten to a place of complete acceptance within myself. Thank you for being my greatest teachers of all.

Morrighan Lynne
January 2018

About the Author

Morrighan Lynne has been a professional psychic medium, intuitive coach, teacher, radio show host, and ordained minister for the past 12 years. When she's not being a Spiritual Rockstar, she enjoys painting mandala art, creating steampunk jewelry and trinkets, and practicing photography. Born in Texas, she has also lived in Arizona and is currently residing in  Idaho with the love of her life, Jonathan. They now live in the Boise area with their two kitties, Luka and Flash.

Happy Accidents

Critically-acclaimed comedy group Four Day Weekend is the longest-running show in the southwest. The group performs a show created from audience suggestions and participation at their 212-seat theater in downtown Fort Worth. They are also celebrating the opening of a new location in Dallas. Voted *Best Comedy* and named *"Best Entertainment Experience in Texas,"* Four Day Weekend is a Fort Worth institution. They've been called *"Fort Worth's Greatest Ambassadors"*, have been awarded the Key to the City, and have performed for two U.S. presidents and delivered a keynote address to the United States Congress.

Following up their comedic success three of the founders of Four Day Weekend have co-written a National Bestselling book,

Happy Accidents: The Transformative Power of "Yes, and" at Work and in Life

For more information visit www.fourdayweekend.com

929 Publishing

6568 S Federal Way
#319
Boise, ID 83716

www.929publishing.com

Be Seen, Be Heard, Be in Print